W9-BQI-107

*TWAYNE'S WORLD AUTHORS SERIES*

*A Survey of the World's Literature*

# SPAIN

Janet W. Diaz, Texas Tech University

and Gerald E. Wade

EDITORS

*The Spanish Sacramental Plays*

TWAS 572

**CALIX DOMINI NOSTRI JESU-CHRISTI**

EX LAPIDE PRETIOSO ACHATE ORIENTALI CORNERINO.

*Ecce icon aere ad vivum exculpta sacrosanctum illum Calicem repraesentans, quo Dominum Nostrum Jesum Christum in suprema nocte mirabile sui sanguinis sacramentum instituisse, eumque à fortissimo Levita Sancto Lau: rentio Roma in Hispaniam missum, traditione majorum accipimus; qui quidem in sancta Metropolitana Eccle: sia Valentina, cui Rex Alfonsus V. dono dedit, et diligentissime asservatur; et maxima colitur religione.*

Original engraving by
Francisco Jordán

# THE SPANISH
# SACRAMENTAL PLAYS

### By RICARDO ARIAS

*Fordham University*

## TWAYNE PUBLISHERS
### A DIVISION OF G. K. HALL & CO., BOSTON

Published in 1980 by Twayne Publishers,
A Division of G. K. Hall & Co.
All Rights Reserved

Printed on permanent/durable acid-free paper and bound
in the United States of America

*First Printing*

Frontispiece engraving by Francisco Jordán ©
Courtesy of the Hispanic Society of America

**Library of Congress Cataloging in Publication Data**

Arias, Ricardo, fl. 1976–
The Spanish Sacramental Plays.

(Twayne's world authors series; TWAS 572)
Bibliography: p. 167–71
Includes index.
1. Christian drama, Spanish—History and criticism.
2. Spanish drama—Classical period, 1500–1700—History
and criticism. 3. Lord's Supper in literature.
I. Title.
PQ6121.R3A7        862'.051        79–25112
ISBN 0–8057–6414–3

To  Carolyn

# Contents

# About the Author

Ricardo Arias completed his undergraduate studies in Spain and in Italy. He received his M. S. in Ed. from Fordham University in 1962, and his Ph.D. in Spanish from New York University in 1968. That same summer he was named a Fellow at the Southeastern Institute of Medieval and Renaissance Studies, held at Duke University, N. C., and directed by Prof. Otis H. Green. He was a lecturer at Queens College, N. Y. for two years, and since 1970 has taught both graduate and undergraduate courses at Fordham University, Bronx, N. Y. where he was recently appointed a full professor of Spanish.

Literature of the Middle Ages and the religious theater of the sixteenth and seventeenth centuries have been his areas of concentration. In addition to publishing a bilingual anthology of Goliardic poetry, and a book on the problems of human destiny in Spanish medieval literature, Dr. Arias has edited a two-volume selection of *autos sacramentales* and is a co-editor of the plays of José de Valdivielso.

His articles have appeared in the *Boletín de la Biblioteca de Menéndez Pelayo, Cuadernos Hispanoamericanos, Revista de Archivos, Bibliotecas y Museos*, in the *Actas del V Congreso Internacional de Hispanistas* and in the *Homenaje* to Prof. R. A. Molina.

# Preface

The *autos sacramentales* or sacramental plays are one of the most intriguing and perplexing manifestations of Spanish literature. They deal by and large with man's moral world, that is, with the workings of his spiritual faculties and senses, as well as with his passions and desires as they affect his capacity to make moral judgments related to a very specific system of values. The psychology of the *autos* is basically the psychology of the medieval moralist, and it should seem simple to us today. More complicated, perhaps even exotic, is the world view present to a greater or lesser extent in every *auto*. In the first two sections of Chapter 1, I attempt to give a summary of the basic doctrines necessary for understanding the content of the plays. I stress the close relationship between the liturgy of the Church and the world of the eucharistic theater. This theater was a consequence of the feast of Corpus Christi, whose history and celebration are described in other sections of the first chapter.

In Chapters 2 and 3, I begin by examining the Eucharist in Spain, from the end of the fifteenth century to the middle of the next one, particularly its popularity as the theme of sermons, silver and gold work, poetry, and other religious writings. All this makes the appearance of the Eucharist in the theater seem a natural phenomenon.

I attempt, in the remaining chapters, to stay within a certain chronological order of authors and plays, but find this difficult at times. Timoneda could probably be included in Chapter 4. Also there are large numbers of plays, anonymous or otherwise, whose dates have not been critically established. Considering the large number of *autos* with a eucharistic theme, I try to limit my comments to the best ones. I judge this selective approach to be the best way to avoid making this book a mere list of names and titles. For those who would like more information, I recommend Flecniakoska's rather complete survey up to Calderón.[1] For each author or collection of works studied, I endeavor to provide at least a minimum of background. My objective in the analysis of each individual play is to establish and evaluate the success with which the author presents some aspect of the eucharistic theme.

And why the eucharistic theme? Perhaps this is the moment to explain what I think the *auto sacramental* is. The many definitions which exist indicate the difficulty of describing a rich genre in a short sentence.[2] Instead of a definition, I prefer a description. None of the authors of *autos* gives us a definition. Calderón makes many observations on the theory of the genre and in the introduction to *La Segunda Esposa y Triunfar Muriendo*,[3] provides a description which I will explain and thereby make mine. A shepherd says that *autos* are "Sermons in verse; questions taken from sacred theology and written for the stage, which my rational faculties can neither explain nor understand. Our exhuberant joy has arranged them in honor and praise of this day."

[Spanish Text.] "Sermones / puestos en verso, en idea / representable cuestiones / de la Sacra Teología, / que no alcanzan mis razones / a explicar ni comprender, / y el regocijo dispone / en aplauso de este día."

*Autos are sermons.* Sermons are part of the liturgy. Their ultimate purpose is to move the will of the audience principally through instruction. The end is not to convince our reason or to give us aesthetic pleasure, but to move our will. The *autos* differ, then, from other kinds of drama. *These sermons are written for the stage.* They use the resources of drama: dialogue, personification, rhetorical devices, and stage scenery. They have only one act. *Autos deal with questions taken from sacred theology.* Theology must be understood in these plays in its widest sense, not as dogmatic theology which deals primarily with the metaphysical formulation of revealed truths. Here, theology is synonymous with the history of salvation, as will be explained later. This of course does not mean that dogmas are not referred to or that the specific language of dogmatic theology is not frequently used.

*Autos present questions which reason can neither explain nor understand.* This is so because they refer to God's mysterious design, ultimately incomprehensible to us and acceptable only on faith. The logic of the *autos* is the logic of faith, a peculiar kind of logic, indeed. One cannot understand the dynamics of the sacramental plays unless this principle is kept in mind. *Autos are in honor and praise of this day.* The Eucharist is the proper theme of these plays. As mentioned earlier, Calderón calls them sermons. A sermon in honor of a saint or of some other festivity has as its theme that saint or that festivity. A Corpus Christi sermon therefore would naturally deal with some aspect of the Eucharist. I realize that this is not the only possible interpretation of the sentence. It is also well known that many plays performed on the Corpus Christi feast were not eucharistic but merely religious. However, in the case of Calderón, my interpretation seems to be correct. All of his *autos* have the Eucharist as their theme.

The presence of these elements in each particular piece varies considerably. In applying these criteria to any particular work, caution and aesthetic common sense should be used. A passing reference to the Eucharist is not enough, but then neither is it necessary for the eucharistic theme to be present throughout. The same is true of allegory. Although there is no mention of allegory in Calderón's description, he makes many observations elsewhere regarding allegory as the proper technique of the *auto*. In some *autos* it may seem rather negligible, while others are totally allegorical.

An area somewhat neglected in this study is the staging of the plays. It was a conscious decision on my part, forced by space limitations. I firmly believe, however, that this aspect is absolutely necessary for a complete presentation of the *autos*. I give the interested reader, in the final bibliography, the necessary references to explore this area on his own. It is my hope that this and other shortcomings will not diminish in the reader the desire for a closer knowledge of these works so appealing both for their brevity and the unusual beauty of so many of them.

I want to express my sincere thanks to many friends for their advice and encouragement. I am particularly grateful to my colleague and friend John Devlin for his patient reading of the manuscript and the many improvements he suggested with his usual ability and good humor. Special thanks are also given to the librarians of Fordham University for their generous help in securing the necessary materials at every step of this project, and to Fordham's Office of Reseach Services for their financial aid in preparing this manuscript.

RICARDO ARIAS

*Fordham University*

# Chronology

1246  Feast of Corpus Christi instituted at Liège, Belgium.

1264  Pope Urban IV extends the feast to the whole church in his bull, *Transiturus*. Thomas Aquinas writes the liturgy for the festivity.

1311  Pope Clement V confirms the celebration at the Council of Vienna.

1314  First observance of the feast in Spain at Gerona.

1317  Pope John XXII adds the procession to the feast.

1319  First documented Corpus procession at Barcelona.

1418  Procession already established at Toledo.

1419  Pope Martin V grants indulgences to those participating in the procession.

1482  First reference to a Corpus procession in Madrid.

1508  Publication of Montesino's *Cancionero* in Toledo.

1516– Reign of King Charles I of Spain.
1556

1517  Beginning of the Protestant Reformation.

1520(?) Yanguas writes the *Farsa sacramental*, the first *auto*.

1551  The bishops at the Council of Trent (1545–1563) give new impetus to the celebration.

1554  Sánchez de Badajoz's *Recopilación en metro* is published in Seville.

1558  Timoneda's *Ternario spiritual* is published in Valencia.

1561  Madrid becomes the capital of Spain.

1574  First reference to the staging of *autos* in Madrid.

1586  From this year on, the *autos* in Madrid are to be staged in the afternoon.

1592  The number of *autos* in Madrid is fixed at four. Two carts are used for each *auto*.

1604  Publication of Lope's *El peregrino en su patria* in Seville, containing four of his earliest *autos*.

1622  Publication of Valdivielso's *Doze actos* in Toledo.

1647 The number of *autos* in Madrid is reduced to two. Four carts are used for each.

1648– All the *autos* performed in Madrid were written by Cal-
1681 derón.

1677 Calderón publishes his *Autos sacramentales, alegóricos e historiales* in Madrid.

1681 Calderón dies.

1749 Nasarre criticizes the *autos* for their mixture of the sacred and profane.

1762 Clavijo y Fajardo attacks the *autos* for their irreverence.

1765 King Charles III forbids the staging of *autos* in Spain.

CHAPTER 1

# The Feast and Its Celebration

THE sacramental plays were written and performed to en-
hance the public celebration of a religious feast. Since the
plays are closely linked to the spirit and the theme of the feast,
the present chapter will be a brief study of those aspects of the
celebration considered important to the understanding of the
*autos.* The institution of the feast of Corpus took place in the
thirteenth century, rather late in the history of Catholic worship.
All the main characteristics of that worship had been developed
centuries before. To better comprehend the place of the feast of
Corpus in the Church's worship, I will outline briefly what
Catholic worship is and how it is organized, leaving a more
complete explanation of its nature and scope for section II of
this chapter.

Catholic worship is the way the church pays homage to God
and, through public prayer and action, brings about the sanctification of her members. The most important act of worship is
the Mass because in it the Last Supper and Christ's death on the
cross are reenacted in a special bloodless way. Here also, the
Christian partakes of the sacrament of the Eucharist in Holy
Communion, and commits himself to His service until he dies.
The Mass is the very center and the principal act of Catholic
worship. It is a memorial of Christ's passion and death. Since
His entire life was a preparation for those moments, it is also,
therefore, a memorial of his entire life. The period before
Christ was a preparation for his coming; thus, the Mass is also
the culmination of all that preceded Christ. With Christ's sacrifice began the "latter days" and the Mass is the act of worship
par excellence in this final period in the history of the world.
Thus, in this sense, we can say that past, present, and future
meet in a very special way in the Mass.

15

Even though this all-embracing dimension is an essential aspect of the Mass, the church has seen fit to divide the yearly cycle of her worship in three parts, during which the faithful are asked to relive, as it were, in a spiritual way the period before Christ, that of his life, and the period after him. The first period called the season of Advent, occurs just before Christmas. The second encompasses Christmas and Easter. The third, the season of Pentecost, commences fifty days after Easter and lasts until Advent. The fact that in this tripartite division only about six months are used to cover the life of Christ was an element that created some serious problems. For instance, the institution of the Eucharist at the Last Supper, or the shedding of Christ's blood, or the piercing of his side by the soldier should all naturally be part of the high days of Holy Week. But the devotion of the faithful for these events grew so strong in later times that special days were set apart, usually outside the period in which they originally fell. A new religious service was created to celebrate these events. This is the origin of the feasts of the Precious Blood, of the Sacred Heart, and of Corpus Christi. By taking them out of the period in which they occurred they were freed from their historical context, so to speak, and from the spiritual mood proper to it. Thus in the three feasts just mentioned the gloom and sadness of Holy Week has been replaced by a joyous fervor that emphasizes the positive spiritual meaning of the events, free from the circumstances of their occurrence.

I    *The Institution of the Feast*

The celebration of the Eucharist, the Mass, is the central focus of the worship of the Church. This fact would seem to be quite adequate to satisfy the devotion of the faithful toward this mystery. However, during the first half of the thirteenth century, there were some religious circles in Liège, Belgium, whose members expressed the wish to celebrate annually a special feast in honor of the Eucharist.[1] Sister Julienne, religious superior of the Cistercian monastery of Mont-Cornillon, acted as their representative. During the summer of 1246, acquiescing to Sister Julienne, Bishop Robert de Torote decided to establish the feast. But the project never materialized. Next, the papal representative, Hugues de Saint-Cher, passing through Liège and obviously pressured by the same people, decreed on December 29, 1252 that the feast should be celebrated in the territories of his legation in Germany. The decree was not very successful.

In August 1261, Urban IV was elected pope. He had been Archdeacon of Campine in Liège and was very sympathetic to the ideas of Julienne of Mont-Cornillon. On August 11, 1264 he mandated the celebration of the feast for the universal Church in the papal bull, *Transiturus*.[2] But Urban IV died soon after and the new feast did not prosper, although it survived in the Germanic countries. Almost a half century passed before Pope Clement V decided to revive the idea. He had the bull, *Transiturus*, reconfirmed by the Council of Vienna in 1311–1312, and the feast was made obligatory everywhere. It is interesting to note that the kings of France, England, and Aragon were present at this council. In 1317 Pope John XXII promulgated the decrees of the Council of Vienna, together with the documents relating to the feast, adding a very important provision of his own: that on that day each parish should celebrate a solemn procession in which the Blessed Sacrament should be carried through the streets, so that it could be publicly worshipped by all. From this moment on, the feast of Corpus Christi was universally celebrated. Two centuries later, it received new impetus during the Council of Trent (1545–1563). On October 11, 1551, the decrees of Urban IV, Clement V, and John XXII were reconfirmed, and the solemn celebration was encouraged as an answer to many Protestant teachings.

From the preceding observations, two facts should be kept in mind: Urban IV's bull, *Transiturus*, was a very lyrical statement concerning the benefits which man receives through the worship and reception of the Eucharist. The underlying feeling is one of unrestrained joy and thanksgiving for this most magnificent of God's gifts. A characteristic mood was established which would influence the tone and spirit of the *autos*. The second fact is the presence of the King of Aragon at the Council of Vienna. The Corpus Christi procession took on a very prominent character in the cities of his kingdom, Gerona, Barcelona, and Valencia, earlier than in the rest of Spain. I am inclined to see in this monarch and his successors enthusiastic promoters of the feast.

Another aspect of the feast, of far greater interest for the study of the *autos* involves the Liturgical Office of Corpus, that is, the prayers, hymns, readings, and other texts arranged in honor of the festivity. Urban IV asked Thomas Aquinas to prepare the office. The result is a magnificent statement of religious joy and theological precision. It is composed of a rich and varied series of biblical texts, beautiful hymns, prayers, instructional readings, and frequent outbursts of joy, all expressing the multiplicity of feelings the faithful experience before Christ present in the Bread of Life. The Divine Office has different parts celebrated at different hours, beginning with the first vespers on the eve of the feast and ending with the vespers of the day. Since Corpus was given the character of a major celebration from the beginning, its duration was extended for eight consecutive days; that is, an octave was added. The Divine Office is an expression of religious worship and presupposes a sincere faith in the Christian who uses it. It is not written in the style of a treatise which tries to teach, although it may incidentally do so. Indeed, it is possible to extract from the texts of the office a summary of the most important teachings about the Blessed Sacrament. To give the reader an idea of the richness of topics and themes which appear in the Liturgy of Corpus and which will be found countless times later on in the *autos*, I will list the following, not in the order in which they appear in the Liturgy, but under these convenient headings.[3]

*The Eucharist and the Old Testament.* Christ is a priest forever, according to the order of Melchizedek. Christ's death and the Eucharist were prefigured in the sacrifice of Isaac, in the Paschal Lamb, and in the manna.

*The superiority of the new order.* The Israelites sacrificed a kid on the eve of the Passover, but our Passover sacrifice is Christ himself. The Bread of the Eucharist is far superior to the bread given by Moses. Elijah was able to walk to the mountain of God after eating the hearth cake, but whoever eats the Bread of the Eucharist will live forever. The Israelites tired of the food (manna) sent by God, but the Bread Christ is His own flesh for the life of the world. The Israelites ate the manna and died, but those who eat this bread will live forever.

*With Christ's sacrifice, the old dispensation ended and the new began.* This idea is repeated several times in different ways. The thought is always the same: The old law was completed; let the new one now follow.

*The Eucharist is a memorial of Christ's wonderful deeds*, especially of his sacrifice on the cross. He instituted the Eucharist because he wants man to share in His divinity. However, we must receive it with the right disposition: for the evil man, it is a source of damnation; for the good, it is a banquet where his energies are renewed to defend himself against the attacks that confront him on every side.

*Faith is a better guide than our senses* in dealing with this mystery, for faith accepts as true that which we can neither see nor understand.

*The Eucharist is a token of our life in heaven.* This idea is expressed forcefully on several occasions. Perhaps the most beautiful is the antiphon: "O sacred banquet, in which Christ is consumed, the memory of His passion is renewed, the mind is filled with grace, and a pledge of future glory is given to us." The Eucharist is the beginning of a new life which will find its culminating expression in heaven. The first prayer of the Mass reads: "Lord Jesus Christ, you gave us the Eucharist as the memorial of your suffering and death. May our worship of this sacrament of your Body and Blood help us to experience the salvation you won for us and the peace of the Kingdom where you live with the Father and the Holy Spirit." The strong desire of the faithful to reach the fullness of life of which the Eucharist is the beginning is expressed in the last prayer: "Lord Jesus Christ, you gave us your Body and Blood in the Eucharist as a sign that even now we share your life. May we come to possess it completely in the Kingdom where you live forever and ever." In addition, in one of the antiphons we find the verse from Rev. 2:17: "To the victor I will give the hidden manna."

*Joy is the natural feeling before the Eucharist.* The Liturgy of Corpus is full of expressions of gladness, from the frequent use of the word "alleluia" to phrases like "praise the Lord," "let our praise be full and resounding," "sing the mystery of the bread and wine," "let those who eat at the table of the Lord resound with shouts of joy," etc.

The Liturgy was undoubtedly one of the main sources of themes and topics for the authors of the *autos*. It is true that theological treatises on the Eucharist were more complete in terms of doctrine. But the *autos* are closer in spirit to the Liturgy than to the somewhat dry expositions of the theologians. The sacramental plays never lose sight of the happiness which pervade the Liturgy of Corpus. They are part of a cheerful celebration. Some of them at times may become theological debates, and certain passages may seem dry, speculative tracts, but these are the exceptions rather than the rule.

## II  *The Liturgy and the* Autos

The feast of Corpus Christi is first and foremost a liturgical celebration, a fact extremely important for any real understanding of the *autos*. These representations were, in fact, part of the religious worship of the day. Hence, it is necessary to have some familiarity with the basic structure of the liturgy in general, and more specifically the Liturgy of Corpus Christi. Thus, in the next few pages I will attempt to offer an outline of the nature and purpose of the Catholic liturgy. The liturgy of the Church has been defined as "the complexus of the sensible, efficacious signs of the Church's sanctification and of her worship."[4] It consists of many different parts: prayers, sermons, songs, gestures, and ceremonies. These are all understood and used as signs, that is, they do not have complete meaning in themselves; they indicate, they suggest, they point to a reality of a higher order beyond them. These signs are sensible, exterior, and perceivable by our senses; and they are efficacious, that is, they do what they signify. For example, the pouring of water in baptism is not just a symbol of purification; it actually cleanses the soul of the baptized from Original Sin.

This brings us to the last part of the definition. This complexus of signs has a twofold purpose: the spiritual improvement of the members of the Church, and the giving of proper honor and reverence to God, who in the final analysis is the origin and ultimate purpose of everything. The signs of the liturgy have not just any value but "a religious value" (Vagaggini, p. 43). As true signs it can be said of them, and consequently of the whole liturgy, that "one thing is seen and another understood."[5] For instance, a group of people at worship can be considered as a sign: "It is a sensible expression of those secret, invisible relations which obtain between God and mankind in the regime of Grace in Christ" (Vagaggini, p. 43).

The precise meaning of all these signs is ultimately determined by God and the Church. They are not natural signs, as smoke is a natural sign of fire. They are real and free signs. As such they contain a certain element of arbitrariness, and the man without faith may reject them as childish. But for the believer they have a precise meaning contained in the Bible and in the teachings of the Church. Ultimately, this is so because God wants it that way, because he "has willed and does will such a regime in the relations between Himself and men" (Vagaggini, p. 61). This regime is what the theologians call the incarnate way. that is, God's will to communicate himself to men and men to God by means of other men and tangible things (Vagaggini, p. 62). Writers of *autos* and spiritual writers in general do not always follow the strict interpretations of the liturgical signs. They very often show a considerable amount of freedom and indeed ingenuity in the interpretation of signs, things, and events. This tendency goes back to the beginning of the Christian era; it flourished during the Middle Ages, and in Spain it continued to the end of the Golden Age. Two outstanding examples in Spanish literature are Berceo's *The Sacrifice of the Mass (El Sacrificio de la Misa)* and Calderón's *auto, The Mysteries of the Mass (Los Misterios de la Misa)*.[6]

Since God wants to communicate himself to us through signs, we can conclude that the history of salvation, sacred history, as contained in the Bible "is based wholly on the concept of sign, both the sign which is speech and the signs which are things or persons" (Vagaggini, p. 62). God's plan of salvation has an intrinsic and deep unity: "The very things and persons about whom the words of Scripture are written have intrinsic reference also, in the designs of God, to other sacred realities" (Vagaggini, p. 63). Everything in God's plan is related to everything else. This relationship is not a static one, but one governed by an intrinsic dynamism according to which each successive phase represents an advance, a progress toward a final goal.

Let me illustrate this point with an example which can be traced back to the early Fathers and which occurs many times in the *autos*. God's relationship to mankind is described as having three successive stages called laws. The natural law is that period in which the relationship was based on two guiding principles instilled by God in man's heart: love of God and love of neighbor. It corresponds historically to the period from Adam to Moses, and was a time of preparation for the next phase, that of the written law. In this second phase the two precepts were not abolished but were expanded to form the Ten Commandments. Calderón expressed the relationship between the two phases as that of a tree to its branches. The written law lasted till the coming of Christ when the law of grace began. In it the two precepts, love of God and love of neighbor, became again the two fundamental rules but in a totally new and far superior context. This is because Christ himself produced them in such a way that he became the central point of God's revelation.

A cautionary word is perhaps in order here. When I say that persons and things in sacred history have the value of signs, I do not want to diminish in any way their historicity, their character as historical facts, established as such by historical methods. I mean rather that those elements are not secular history but sacred history. Therefore, they possess an extra dimension derived from the total plan of which they are a part with very special relationships to all the other parts. The fact toward which persons and events in sacred Scripture aimed and for which they were a preparation was Christ. He is the climax of sacred history, the One who gives it its intrinsic and real unity. And he does this in such a way that everything "before Him tends to Him . . . and that after Him everything derives from Him" (Vagaggini, p. 15). This principle cannot be stressed enough, for it provides the clue to our proper understanding of the nature of the liturgy. The signs of the liturgy and especially of the Mass are a synthesis and a mirror in which, as Vagaggini says, "are reflected and gathered as real and present all the relationships between God and man; rather, between

God and the world in general which constitute sacred history"
(Vagaggini, p. 91).

This becomes clearer perhaps if I explain a little further some
of the principles already mentioned. The unity and dynamism
of God's plan is the basis for the relationship between its different aspects and also for the fuller meaning and higher quality
of each successive stage. Thus, persons and events of the Old
Testament can be viewed as signs of future persons and events.
Once the thing signified has been fulfilled, those early signs
acquire a deeper meaning and transcendent reality over and
above the purely historical one, for they can now be viewed as
already containing, inchoatively, the persons and events of suc-
ceeding periods, that is, the things signified by them. For instance, in the light of Christ's death, the story of God's command
to Abraham to sacrifice Isaac becomes a sort of first draft of
Christ's death on the cross. The offering of bread and wine to
Abraham by the priest Melchizedek becomes a foreshadowing
of Christ the Priest and the Eucharist. The manna sent by God
to the Israelites in the desert is the sign par excellence of the
eucharistic bread.[7]

In the *autos* the first of the two things related is usually called
a sign, type, figure, shadow, or rough draft of the second one,
that is, the thing signified; each stage was a preparation for the
next, and in its turn each successive phase was in a certain
sense present in the previous one, "in the way that the rough
cast makes the future statue really present, though inchoatively . . ." or ". . . as the statue actualizes and makes present
the rough cast which it realizes and from which it was prepared."[8]

This method of interpretation was used constantly in the New
Testament in relation to the Old Testament. Christ was viewed
as the fulfillment of all the signs of the Old Testament. Christ
used this method Himself when He joined the two disciples on
the way to Emmaus. If the Old Testament tended toward the
New as to its fulfillment, the same can be said of Christ's earthly
life in relation to his death on the cross. "The Cross . . . sums
up and fulfills in itself all the preceding redemptive actions of
Christ's life. . . . In fact, Christ's whole earthly life is but one
redemptive mystery which is fulfilled on the Cross."[9] The au-

thors of *autos* often established different relationships between moments of His life: for example, the first spilling of His blood during the circumcision was compared with the blood on the cross, and the multiplication of the loaves with the institution of the Eucharist.

Christ's redemptive work ended with the cross, but God's plan did not end there. "Golgotha itself tended with all its momentum to the resurrection, ascension, sitting at the Father's right hand and sending of the Spirit at Pentecost, because only (then) . . . did Christ gather for Himself and for us the fruits of Golgotha and communicate them to us" (Vagaggini, pp. 111–2). An awareness of the multiple relationships which can thus be established between persons and events of the Old and New Testaments, and between the different moments of Christ's own life should help us considerably in understanding what would otherwise seem an arbitrary and meandering train of thought in so many *autos*. For, while it is true that sometimes the relationships they established were based on poetical rather than sound, exegetical reasons, generally speaking, they followed the latter method of interpretation.

The last phase of God's plan toward man is realized now in the society instituted by Christ, the Church. It is very much in agreement with the incarnate way God chose to follow. The Church participates in the nature of a sign for it is "the human and divine, visible and invisible, spiritual and yet socially structured framework of life" (Vagaggini, p. 16) founded by Christ. He entrusted to her all the necessary means to carry on his redemptive work, especially by means of the seven sacraments. They are also sensible, exterior, and efficacious signs through which he gives us spiritual life. Each one of these signs "as effective commemorative sign of Christ's historical redemptive actions, actualizes presentially . . . all mysteries of Christ's life from the Incarnation to the Cross to the resurrection and to Pentecost" (Vagaggini, p. 112). While this is true of every sacrament, it is much more so of the Eucharist, for in it "the very person of Christ, and not only His supernatural power, is really present in His divinity and in His full, glorious humanity" (Vagaggini, p. 110).

A very important aspect of the sacraments that should be

mentioned here and which has great bearing on the aesthetics of the *auto* is their character as prophetic signs. Just as persons and events of the Old Testament, for example, were prophetic signs of things to come, so too the sacraments effectively actualize the future and Second Coming of Christ (Vagaggini, p. 112). After Christ's actions were completed, the "latter days" (eschatological time) began. Nothing new would be added to God's plan of salvation. However, its final culmination and fulfillment would take place only with the passing of the regime of signs, "with the glorious return of the Lord and the passage into eternity" (Vagaggini, p. 15) when we will see God face to face. The last scenes of the *autos* usually end with the glorification of the Eucharist as a commemorative sign and, equally important, as a prophetic sign of these ultimate realities.[10]

I have considered up to now the predominant aspect under which the liturgy presents Catholic doctrine. It does not present it as a set of clearly defined dogmas or metaphysical principles, but as a history of God's actions and interventions in the world. This is the way the Bible presented it, and this is the way the liturgy does also. However, it is perfectly legitimate to explore with our reason, guided by faith, what those facts mean and to organize those conclusions in a certain system. This is what theology, more specifically dogmatic theology, does. While the *autos* followed rather closely the way of the liturgy, they often made use of concepts and words proper to the dogmatic treatises on the Eucharist. Only well-annotated editions of the plays can provide explanations of all these technical terms.

I will limit myself here to a brief outline of the history of salvation, constantly present in the *autos*. It is divided into three phases: eternity, time, and eternity.

*Eternity.* The first phase corresponds to the life of the Trinity before time: Father, Son, and Holy Spirit. They are three persons in one nature, equal in dignity but different in their manifestations toward man. They create the angels. Some rebel against God: The good angels follow Michael, the bad choose Lucifer.

*Time.* The Trinity shares its life with visible creatures: creation of the world and Adam as its master, a state of perfect harmony, the first parents tempted by the fallen angel, the Fall or Original Sin, the beginning of the cosmic struggle between good and evil, the promise of the Redeemer, the preparation for His coming, Christ's redemption, and the last times.

*Eternity.* This last phase depicts the damnation of the bad and the inauguration of the kingdom of God in heaven.

Although the three phases are not mentioned in every *auto*, they are certainly presupposed. The three persons of the Trinity appear in the plays often. Since they are equal and indivisible, in some *autos* the same character assumes functions which we normally would associate with two separate characters. In Calderón's *The Divine Orpheus* (*El Divino Orfeo*), for example, Orpheus plays the role of Creator (Father) and Redeemer (Christ). The rebellion of the evil angels is mentioned in innumerable plays, often in lengthy passages of great literary beauty. Since Lucifer was the principle of evil, he appears under many names: Satan, Devil, Night, or as any of the seven capital sins. Quite often he appears himself in addition to one or several sins or vices, as different aspects of himself.[11] The presence of the Devil looms large because of his role in the temptation and Fall of Adam. By accepting the Devil's suggestions, Adam lost the state of perfect happiness for himself and all his descendants. This story provided a simple outline easily transferable to the fall of any man after him, that is, to any sinner. It also offered all the elements for excellent drama.

Some of the most moving passages in the *autos* concern precisely these moments: man, created in God's image, rebels against Him, soils and erases that image to live in a state of wretchedness from which only God's love can save him. With the promise of a Redeemer, God's love shows its extraordinary qualities. Man or his soul is often described as God's bride or spouse. Should God abandon her on account of her unfaithfulness? That would not do for a true lover. He will come back and give such proofs of His love as to win her back. Not only will He die, but He will even remain in the Sacrament. The Devil, however, will not give up but will try to take her away. Her ultimate fate will be decided by her attitude toward this last proof of His love after His death: the Eucharist.

The struggle between good and evil is present at all moments of God's plan. It is a struggle of cosmic proportions. Satan's rebellion divided the angels. Adam's Fall created disharmony in creation. Christ's triumph makes possible our liberation and also that of the material world, from Satan. In his *auto, Life Is A Dream (La Vida Es Sueño)* Calderón gave this idea a beautiful poetic form by making the four elements pay homage to the Eucharist at the play's end. The Eucharist appears here again as the central point in God's plan. It could not be otherwise, given the fact that, under the veil of Bread and Wine, Christ and consequently the Trinity are really present. St. Paul expressed this forcefully by saying "A man should examine himself first; only then should he eat of the bread and drink of the cup. He who eats and drinks without recognizing the body eats and drinks a judgment on himself."

Let me summarize what has been stated up to this point. First, divine revelation as it is presented in the Bible, appears as a history, as sacred history. "It is not metaphysics or morality . . . that predominates, but history, with a metaphysical background and a moral derivation which is powerfully brought out" (Vagaggini, p. 4). This is the way it also appears in the liturgy and in the sacramental plays. The Bible, the liturgy, and the plays presuppose a believing audience, that is, an audience with the gift of faith. The Bible and the liturgy present their moral teaching in terms of certain facts, certain actions or interventions freely taken by God, and from which they derive some guiding principles. The sacramental plays, even those which seem most argumentative and polemic, rest ultimately on a set of facts or principles which are taken on faith. Flecniakoska expressed this very well: "The purpose of these works . . . is to remind the spectators, in an entertaining way, of what they have previously admitted to know" very well.[12] The many instances in which the authors want to argue or prove one thing or another are never more than simple illustrations taken from ordinary life or nature. They don't prove much, but they are enough to elicit a moral and a devotional reaction from the audience.[13]

Second, the sacred history presented by the *autos* is of a very special nature. God himself is the director, and for this reason it possesses a supratemporal unity, manifested in the special relationships which the different phases have among themselves. Even though God's plan manifests itself in a certain chronological order, this aspect is of secondary importance to us now. For instance, even though the Trinity or the specific manner of our redemption by Christ was not revealed until the New Testament, authors of the *autos* presented it as already operative in the moment of Creation or at the Fall of Man. These are not poetic flights of the imagination but sound examples of exegesis. Because every phase of God's plan contains others to come, as in a rough cast, very often the dramatist can choose for the subject of his plays some person or event, and present it as a true eucharistic theme, with minor subtle touches that make its meaning clear and precise.

Third, because Christ is the central point of God's plan toward which everything tends, and because he chooses to remain really present in the Eucharist, this Sacrament is consequently the most important one. All the other sacraments tend towards it and derive their meaning and power from it. It is the center around which revolves the life of the Church and its members. Furthermore, all the precepts and the entire moral code are built around it.

Fourth, since the success of God's plan depends ultimately on our positive collaboration, on our free will giving its assent, and on our choice between good and evil, the *autos* very frequently dramatized, with extraordinary force and beauty, the process of man's faculties arriving at a decision. It was in this fine psychological analysis of man's moral world that moments of true drama were created. The stakes were always high, for in this process man's ultimate fate was decided. The authors displayed an intimate and profound knowledge of man's psychology in his struggle between the attractions of the senses and that of higher spiritual values. They gave us very realistic descriptions of man's present condition, a composite of body and soul, flesh and spirit, debating between the visible realities and the invisible spiritual ones still hidden under the veil of signs.

Fifth, since God's plan and his interventions are all inspired by love, it is only natural that the relationship between God and man can be portrayed legitimately as that taking place between a lover and his beloved. The multiple forms this relationship can take give the playwright a rich list of possible plots and developments. The Bible, especially the Song of Songs and the Prophets, provided many themes and motifs; so did the mythological stories and classical writers. The contemporary secular theater also provided a large number of topics and motifs. Obviously, the *auto* never suffered from a scarcity of materials.[14]

It is my hope that these observations may help the reader to understand the world of the liturgy, for a working knowledge of it constitutes the best introduction to the world and the doctrine of the *autos*. If the worship of the Church in general revolves around the Eucharist, the Liturgy of the feast of Corpus Christi is completely dedicated to the celebration of this mystery. The Mass and the different parts of the Divine Office of this day present a magnificent summary of the important aspects of the Eucharist in the context of the joy of the feast. From the Liturgy come many of the topics and especially the spirit of joy and celebration so characteristic of the *autos*.

### III   *The Corpus Christi Procession*

In the papal documents establishing the liturgical celebration of Corpus Christi, the idea that the feast should be a joyous and festive occasion is expressed several times. This idea took on a visible form in the solemn procession in which the Blessed Sacrament was carried through cities and villages. Processions were already part of some religious festivities, but the one of Corpus Christi was to eclipse all the others both in the interest with which it was celebrated and in the extraordinary dimensions that it would acquire with the passing of time, especially in the important cities. It was also celebrated in the small villages with less pomp but equal religious fervor and continues up to the present.

For our understanding of the *autos* as literature, the procession is, I think, of secondary importance. Its value consists mainly of the fact that it gives us an idea of the enthusiasm and joy with which the feast was celebrated by ecclesiastics and laity alike. George Very's study of the procession is the most comprehensive. I have used it as the principal source of the following remarks.[15] Pope John XXII in 1317 added an octave and a public procession to the feast (Very, pp. 3, 23). A century later, in 1419, Pope Martin V granted indulgences to those who attended it, seeming to indicate that the procession was an established custom by this time. In Spain several cities claim the honor of having been the first to hold Corpus Christi processions. Barcelona, however, offers solid evidence of the first processions held in 1319, 1320, and 1322. Lérida had one before 1340, Valencia in 1348 or 1355, and Palma de Mallorca in 1371.

In the beginning, each parish had its own procession. Soon after, a single procession was held with the parishes and guilds participating. Romeu Figueras observes that the Corpus Christi procession adopted many of the elements used in the solemn reception of kings and nobles, or in the celebration of important civic events. In Valencia about 1269, during the reign of James I, and in Zaragoza in 1286, during the coronation of Alfonso II, solemn processions were held in which carts were drawn carrying allegorical scenes, accompanied by groups of dancers. Some of these scenes have a close relationship with the sacred representations of the Corpus Christi procession.[16] The hour of the procession varied considerably according to the times and cities, and changed if circumstances so required. In some cities the profane elements were separated from the main procession. They marched the day before or on the same day, but before the main religious event (Very, p. 24). The order of the different elements altered a great deal. We have a rather complete description of the procession in Barcelona in 1424. As Romeu Figueras indicates, it follows the cyclical pattern of a medieval mystery.[17]

First came the scenes contributed by the city council: Creation, hell with Lucifer, the battle of the angels with the devils, Paradise with an angel, Adam and Eve, Cain and Abel, the Ark, Melchizedek, Abraham and Isaac, Lot with his wife and two daughters, Jacob and the angel, David and Goliath, the twelve tribes of Israel. There followed the scenes presented by the cathedral representing Moses and Aaron; the ten prophets; John the Baptist; Susanna and the judges; Daniel and the angels; Judith, Raphael, and Tobias; the Annunciation; the Nativity; the Magi; the Holy Innocents with Rachel; the soldiers;

and King Herod and his advisors. Third came the scenes from the Church of Santa Ana, representing the saints venerated in that church. These were followed by the scenes from the Convent of the Merced representing images of saints, then Mary, Jesus, and Joseph; the risen Christ under the cross; Gestas with his devil; Longinus; Joseph of Arimathea and Nichodemus; twelve angels; the tomb with Mary Magdalene; and the statues of St. Anthony, St. Onophrius, St. Paul the Hermit, and St. Alexis. Finally came the scenes from the Church of St. Eulalia with the images of the saints venerated there (Very, pp. 37–39). The decoration and artistic value of the scenes was significant. To better preserve them, a *casa de las rocas* was built in 1422 with a person put in charge of their upkeep. As the years passed, some of the elements just mentioned were dropped, and new ones made their appearance. In 1589 images of eagles were introduced (Very, p. 31), and in the sixteenth century the fearful *Vibre* (serpent) is also mentioned (Very, p. 40).

The procession in Valencia has characteristics similar to the one in Barcelona. As early as 1410 we find floats or carts depicting scenes from the Bible as well as saints and devils. In 1535 the city council ordered the construction of eight floats to represent the following scenes: Adam and Eve, the Particular Judgment, St. Jerome, the Last Supper, the Descent from the cross, the Holy Sepulcher, the Last Judgment, and the Adoration of the Kings. By 1542 the number of floats had increased and the themes changed. Still later on, the number of floats was reduced to six (Very, p. 27). As early as 1399 we also find figures of large, crowned eagles in addition to the floats. Their symbolism is variously explained as representing the eagle of the Book of Revelation or the devotion to the Sacrament by the Roman and Spanish churches indicated by the letters R.E. on the images (Very, p. 31). The scenes on the floats mentioned previously came to be represented by persons. They also acquired more theatrical aspects by the recitation or singing of texts. But the scenes never lost their character of medieval mystery plays and for that reason failed to contribute anything "to the development of the sacramental play" (Wardropper, p. 53). As Lázaro Carreter says: "It is surprising that in the short texts introduced during the Corpus procession, the Eucharistic themes have so little, if any importance."[18]

Recent discoveries in the archives of the Cathedral of Toledo have established that by 1418 the Corpus Christi procession was the main public event of the festivities there. Carpenters and blacksmiths took care of the litter bier (*andas*) where the Sacrament was carried. Mention is also made of several carts for the organs and images, as well as platforms erected by the carpenters.[19] The documents at Toledo for 1431 list the minstrels who played in the procession. In documents for 1445 we are told of certain *juegos* that took place. According to the two scholars who studied the documents, they are more or less simple representations in which some shepherds took part because they were paid.[20]

An item of great interest has recently been established. The famous writer Alfonso Martínez de Toledo, Arcipreste de Talavera (1398–1466?) was in charge of the preparations for the feast, from 1454 through 1457.[21] The documents for 1456 specifically refer to *representaciones* that were part of the procession and were staged plays.[22] Torroja Menéndez and Rivas Palá believe that many of the Arcipreste's innovations in Toledo were the result of what he had seen in Barcelona and especially in Valencia where he had lived for over ten years.[23] There is no question that he contributed significantly to the splendor of the procession in Toledo, which rivaled those held in the other major cities.[24] Theatrical performances in Toledo soon became very important. The number of plays varied, but by 1493 there were seven plays performed on Corpus Christi.[25]

Until the discoveries at Toledo, Seville enjoyed the honorable reputation of being the first city in western Spain to have a procession. The documented date for Seville is 1454. Processions were apparently celebrated there with great splendor from the very beginning; they became more and more elaborate as the years passed. A rather late document of 1594 provides us with a wealth of information on the rich and varied decorations that the members of the parish of St. Salvador created for the public celebration of the feast. The document pictures for us "a city literally covered with altars, hangings, tapestries, 'inventions', arches of triumph, fountains . . ."[26] The preparations for the celebration started a month before the feast and involved a large number of people. Let us look, for example, at those for the year 1613 (Very, p. 15). The first meeting of the Commission for Corpus took place on March 16. On April 22 it was agreed that there would be seven dances, the same as in previous years, along with the giants and the *tarasca*.[27] The usual prizes were to be given to the best dancers and the best plays. Care was taken in purchasing awnings and pine trees to adorn the route of the procession, and a man was contracted to sweep and water the Plaza Mayor. All the expenses would be paid by the city council. It was also agreed that the dances and the plays would be performed for inspection twenty days before the feast.

On 2 May, two members of the council were requested to contract theatrical troupes for the four *autos*. If they could not be found, the money would be spent on floats. However, three companies were contracted under the following conditions. First, the commission would choose the plays, and they would be performed four times: before the clergy of the cathedral, before the town council, before the royal *audiencia,* and finally, before the people in general. Second, the players would ride on one cart, dressed according to their roles, "the materials to be of velvet, damask and satin, with false passementerie of gold and silver."[28] Third, they had to repeat the plays on the Monday after the feast. Finally, in addition to the *auto*, the troupe was to perform a new interlude (*entremés*). On 5 May all those wanting to present dances or other *invenciones* were invited to the town hall so that the deputies could choose the best ones. Prizes would also be granted to those who had built the three most praiseworthy arches and artistic processional crosses and to those who best decorated the facades of their houses along the processional route (Very, p. 17). On the following day, 6 May, the results were announced.

Hernando Mallero was to present two dances, one called "Joshua" ("Josué") with eighteen dancers plus music and drum, and the other, the "Gypsies" ("Gitanas") with sixteen members plus music and drum. The costumes were approved, and it was also decided that the men in the second dance would wear bells on their legs, colored half-stockings, and white shoes (Very, p. 17). Hernando de Rivera was to provide two dances, the first called "The Strength of Rengo" ("Las Fuerzas de Rengo") with nineteen members, music and drum, and the second, "The Conquest of the Three Nations" ("La Conquista de las Tres Naciones") with eighteen members, music, and drum. Francisco Hernández would perform three dances. The first would be "The Conquest of the Indies" ("La Conquista de las Indias") with sixteen members; the second, "The Peasant of the Danube" ("El Villano del Danubio") with eighteen dancers, music, and drum; and the third, a sword dance with sixteen members plus music, drum, and cymbals.

At the same meeting, a person was appointed to take care of the preparation of the carts; on 14 May the streets and squares to be furnished with awnings were selected. The next day, 15 May, a contest was called for the preparation of the *tarasca* and the giants that would be paraded on the eve of the feast, on the feast itself, and on the octave day (Very, p. 19). A contract was also awarded for the rushes, popular branches, and reeds to be put on the streets; and on 18 May another was drawn to supply pine trees to be set in place two days before the feast.

The entire council met on 1 June to view the four plays to be performed. They were all approved with minor corrections. Two days later the commissions reviewed the dances (Very, p. 20). The town crier took care of the final details. Those living along the route of the procession were to adorn their houses, sweep their frontages, and put down rushes. No chairs were to be placed in front of the houses. Anyone disobeying these orders would be fined accordingly. Finally, traffic was forbidden on those streets "under penalty of confiscation of the coach and 100 lashes to the coachman" (Very, p. 20). In Madrid the procession assumed unusual proportions with an equally complicated system of preparation. The first reference to a Corpus Christi procession at that place is in the year 1482, though one was probably held much earlier (Very, p. 6). A contract for a dance of giants was signed in 1585, and a similar one was drawn in 1609.

It seems that there was a custom of building small altars in front of private houses. Lope de Vega approached the Duque de Sessa in 1611 and again in 1614 asking for help in preparing the ones he was to build in front of his house. In 1623 mention is made of the altars built in front of the palaces of several noblemen (Very, p. 13). There were local variations in the course of time. A dance of seven persons with music from a timbrel, guitar, and a hand-drum appears in 1612; a contract of May 1619 mentions a *tarasca* (Very, p. 15). In 1623 the streets were adorned with tapestries, some from the royal household, representing the wars of Túnez and La Goleta; others told the story of Abraham and Noah (Very, p. 12). That same year the procession started at nine in the morning and ended around three in the afternoon (Very, p. 24). The order of that procession was as follows.

After the *tarasca* and before the monstrance came the members of eight of the governing Councils of the Realm, next "the Chapter General of the clergy, then twenty-four priests vested in copes with thuribles," the clergy of the Royal Chapel, three priests accompanying the archbishop, and the archbishop of Santiago of Compostela. The pages of the king marched afterward, with candles lighted, and after them came the Sacrament. Along the sides walked the members of the city council. The king and his son passed next, followed by Cardinals Zapata and Espínola, the papal nuncio, the bishop of Pamplona, the inquisitor general, the patriarch of the Indies, and ambassadors from Poland, France, Venice, England, and Germany. The last group included the king's favorite, the Conde-Duque de Olivares and a number of grandees (Very, pp. 35–36). It was indeed the most solemn civic and religious event of the year, one in which king and peasant shared alike. The religious nature of the celebration was the binding element which gave unity to such varied participants.

Before I conclude these comments, mention should be made of certain elements in the procession, some of which have an obvious religious significance, while others are more problematic. Among the first are the many motifs from the Old and New Testaments stated as part of the decorations of the streets and buildings and also as themes for the dances. These are found in Valencia in 1412 (Very, pp. 30–31), in Seville in 1595 (Very, p. 12), and again in 1613, and in Madrid in 1623. The procession of 1622, in Segovia, had a dance with the theme of

King Saul and the giant Goliath.[29] In Madrid there was a dance representing the struggle between the angels and the devils, dressed as Moors. It ended with St. Michael decapitating the Mohammedans (Very, p. 21).

More difficult to understand in such a solemn and religious procession is the continued presence of profane and secular details. The *tarasca*, the little devils, the giants, and the many different kinds of secular dances seem to have been a part of the procession from early times. Judging by the frequent references in all kinds of documents, the *tarasca* seems to have been the most popular item. Very thinks its origin is in the dragon-serpent of the Babylonians, Assyrians, and Egyptians. It is mentioned in the Old Testament, and medieval commentators saw it as one of the representations of the Devil (Very, p. 51). The appearance of a dragon in many religious processions is attested to in innumerable sources from the early Christian era (Very, p. 55). The name *tarasca* seems to derive from the old Provençal word *drasca* used around 1213 with the meaning of serpent. It was soon associated with the city of Tarascón where, according to legend, there was a water monster in the river Rhone. This region was converted to Christianity by St. Martha, who overpowered the dragon and brought it to Tarascón. An image of the monster was carried in the procession in honor of the saint, beginning around 1474 (Very, pp. 58–62).

Although the word *tarasca* is found in Spanish for the first time in 1530 in relation to the Corpus procession in Seville (Very, pp. 59, 68), references to a winged dragon used in public celebrations appear much earlier, such as in Valencia in 1392 and 1399. The following year in Valencia, St. Margaret and St. George were introduced in the Corpus procession, together with the dragons they had slain (Very, p. 67). In 1598 a dragon appears in the Corpus procession in Madrid. But the first comprehensive description is given in 1630. It was over ten feet long with wings, three monkeys on its back, and was painted according to the design of Cosme Lotti. It was a figure of fun and symbolism (Very, pp. 66, 69). As the symbolism of the *tarasca* was developed, other figures began to be associated with it. Such was the case with the *tarasquilla* and the little devils (Very, p. 66). The former figure appeared sometimes on the back of the *tarasca* dressed rather daringly, symbolizing Lust or Heresy, and on occasion was referred to as the Ann Boleyn (Very, p. 70). I concur with Bruce Wardropper's observations concerning the Corpus Christi procession. He rightly says that "for the historian of the *auto* the most important aspect of the procession is the allegorical tone which was . . . its initial characteristic (Wardropper, p. 51).

The procession never followed a single pattern in any particular city. It seems that the *tarasca*, the little devils, giants, and dwarfs were first, although in Valencia and Barcelona the floats had this honor (Very, p. 27). After the *tarasca* and floats came "groups of children, the religious orders, parishes, the eagles, Evangelists and other scriptural characters, the guilds with their patron saints and representations of scenes from the life of the saint, the Sacrament on its triumphal cart, or else carried on *andas,* surrounded by dignitaries of the city and the officiating prelate, and guards of honor" (Very, pp. 25–26). In big cities the number of the religious orders was large. In 1623 in Madrid there were eleven orders represented. The number of parishes was even larger (Very, p. 29). The guilds also formed a very important group. In a city as small as Pontevedra we find thirteen different guilds marching in 1658. Very often the guilds carried floats for their patron saints with groups of dancers with musicians on them (Very, pp. 33, 35). The Blessed Sacrament usually came after the guilds. The clergy carried it in a monstrance either on a triumphant cart (*carro triunfal*) or on a stretcher (*andas*). The Host was immediately followed by the officiating prelate and his assistants, and then the high-ranking members of society and the civil authorities. The nucleus around the Blessed Sacrament reached unusual proportions in Madrid, with several groups jealously guarding their place in the procession not only in relation to the King of Heaven and Earth in the monstrance, but in relation to the King of Spain marching among them. Details of the order of the procession of 1623 in Madrid have already been given. Upon returning, the procession usually concluded with a solemn benediction and the singing of the Eucharistic hymn "Tantum Ergo Sacramentum."

The information given above, sketchy and intentionally short, is, I hope, sufficient to give an impression of what the Corpus Christi was like. I would summarize some of its constant characteristics in the following way: the feast was conceived and encouraged by the highest ecclesiastical authorities as a public religious tribute to the Sacrament; its importance is further attested to by the granting of indulgences to those who took part. It was a festive and joyous celebration from which no well-disposed member of the society should be excluded. Very early in its history secular and profane elements made their appearance. Many of them still remain somewhat disconcerting to the modern reader. They were also disturbing to some contemporaries who inveighed against them rather frequently. The *tarasca*, the giants, and the many dances seemed more akin to secular entertainment perhaps than to religious homage to the Sacrament. Thre is no question that many people reacted this way. For others there was always the possibility of justifying the presence of these groups with biblical examples: King David had danced in front of the ark (Very, p. 84).

For those with more of a sense of humor than capacity for interpretation, the procession was an occasion for pranks and practical jokes. By loosening the ropes which held the awnings in Seville, pranksters could scare unwary people out of their wits (Very, p. 13). In Barcelona, in the middle of the sixteenth century, there were serious disturbances caused by rivalry among different guilds. During 1556 the Governor had to put several of the more undisciplined members in prison. In the same city the firing of rockets was so intense and annoying that the bishop had to intervene (Very, p. 40).

The Corpus procession was also an excellent opportunity to indulge in the social pastime of seeing and being seen. The season of the year, the festive air, and the rich decorations provided the best background for exhibiting one's self in the finest possible way, thereby satisfying vanity with the most honorable religious excuse. The cold eye of the moralist saw through this web of deception, however. Fr. Luis de Granada complained in one of his sermons that his contemporaries had made this festivity a display of vanity, even though it was supposed to be strictly spiritual.[30] In a similar vein, Zabaleta described a typical young man: "Finally our splendid young man leaves his home dressed in such a way that if he had any sense he would be more ashamed than if he were naked" (Very, pp. 24, 124). The same author also mentioned that "the women, half of their bodies practically naked, watch from the balconies as the procession passes" (Very, pp. 24, 124). Quiñones de Benavente satirized the opinion of those who saw little difference between the procession and a bullfight: "This is June, a certain month which, being naturally courteous and well-mannered, wants to provide windows and seats for the feast of Corpus and for the bullfight" (Very, p. 124, n. 5).

Other spiritual writers saw in the procession an uninhibited manifestation of religious joy. Saint John of Avila saw it in this context. In one of his writings he says: "Let the people look at it (the Sacrament) with great love; let all those in the streets and from their doors or windows worship Him reverently; let the priest offer Him incense and let the laymen dance before Him with reverent joy, as David did before the Ark" (Very, pp. 84–85). Damián de Vegas wrote in a beautiful poem, published in 1590: "Today is a day of joy, let everyone be happy. It must indeed be a great feast since Christ Himself comes to it disguised. . . . To go about with a sad face today is a sure sign of being out of one's mind. . . . if David . . . danced before the Ark . . . what would he have done before God Himself? He would have leaped for joy all over the streets and squares. . . ."[31] Similar expressions of unrestrained joy are frequent in the plays themselves. Calderón elevated this popular enthusiasm to the category of religious worship. In the *auto, The General Pardon* (*El Indulto General*), David says that "rejoicing is worship as long as it is well-ordered."[32]

CHAPTER 2

# The Eucharist in Nontheatrical Works

THE study of the procession provides a good idea of the attitude with which Spaniards celebrated the feast of Corpus Christi. In this chapter, I will take a brief look at some works (beginning with the end of the fifteenth century and continuing through the sixteenth) which clearly indicate the importance of the Eucharist in other areas such as sermons, silver and gold works, lyric poetry, and devotional writing. This review should help the reader understand the preparation which the average Spaniard could gain from these different sources for understanding not only the significance of the mystery celebrated but also the *autos*. As I will presently show, in all these works there was great similarity of topics, language, and forms, and they were all within reach of the average spectator of the *autos*. Familiarity with these works gave the audience an adequate amount of information to follow and a feeling of enjoyment as he watched the plays presented on the stage.[1]

In spite of the obvious similarities between these works, the present state of research makes it impossible to affirm categorically the influence of one on the other, or of any of them on the *auto*. For the moment, then, let it suffice to show some of the more important nontheatrical manifestations of the eucharistic theme.

## I   *The Eucharist and the Pulpit*

The most accessible and widespread source of information about the Eucharist was probably sermons. Very little research has been done on the relationship between the sermons of Corpus Christi, the sacramental plays, and the public which heard both. During the fifteenth and sixteenth centuries several

40

theoretical treatises on the art of preaching were published.[2] Towards the end of the fifteenth century homiletics "was an integral part of the curriculum in the schools of theology, and . . . the basis of this preaching was the interpretation of Sacred Scripture.[3] A growing number of zealous ecclesiastics took the practice of preaching very seriously. Men like Hernando de Talavera (1428–1507), Dionisio Vázquez (1479–1539), Tomás de Villanueva (1488–1555), Juan de Avila (1500–1560), and Luis de Granada (1504–1588) had established a solid tradition of sacred oratory which was to continue throughout the seventeenth century.

Since the sources of both sermons and plays were the same, namely, the Bible, the liturgy, and the Fathers, the similarities were bound to be many and important. One of the sermons by Father Dionisio Vázquez, a great theologian and the first to occupy the chair of Sacred Scripture at the University of Alcalá, was so fastpaced and had so much dialogue that its modern editor rightly calls it "one of those primitive sacramental plays which jumped from the pulpit to the carts of Corpus."[4] The sermon relied completely on sacred Scripture; no philosophical arguments, no theological speculations, just simple exegesis, comparable to what Christ did with the disciples on the way to Emmaus (Luke 24:13–35).[5] Discussing Christ's death, Vázquez said that God could have saved us some other way since He is omnipotent. But Christ died so that the prophecies would be fulfilled. The salvation He brought us was prefigured in Noah's Ark (pp. 35–38). His death was also prefigured in the sacrifice of Isaac, for "Abraham was a prefiguration of Christ, as far as He was God, since He was obedient to His Father in taking on human flesh. Isaac was a prefiguration of Christ, as man, because he was obedient to his Father unto death" (Vázquez, p. 39). The sermon concludes: "And His passion and death were necessary in order to bring Scripture to a conclusion and to fulfill it and to give glory to humankind" (Vázquez, p. 43).

Fray Luis de Granada, in *The Sermon on the Feast of the Most Blessed Sacrament (Sermón en la Fiesta del Sanctísimo Sacramento)*.[6] stated that the Eucharist was first among all the sacraments because, as St. Thomas said, "In this sacrament Christ our Saviour is present wholly and truly" (de Granada,

p. 23). The Eucharist is also a source of grace for us: "This food is a special remedy instituted by the Lord against that poisonous mouthful which our first parents ate." It is "a certain spiritual nourishment and restoration which the soul receives" (de Granada, p. 23). The Eucharist was most appropriately prefigured in the bread brought by the angel to the prophet Elijah. God wanted to show us the depth of His fatherly love in the sweetness of this sacrament, just as Solomon said He did when God sent the sweet manna to His people (de Granada, p. 24). Allegorically, it does delight the palate of the soul with marvellous sweetness.

The sermon goes on to say that the Eucharist serves to refrain our passions and appetites. The poets told the story of a Sibyl who prepared a certain kind of bread which she gave to Cerberus. He became so tame that he fell asleep, leaving thus the passage free and safe for the travelers. Now this was a fictitious story, but it offers a very useful comparison to help us understand the impressive power of the sacrament and the reason for its institution (de Granada, p. 24). The sacrament gives us strength against our wayward inclinations and evil appetites. This bread was prefigured in that admirable loaf, mentioned in Judges, chapter 7, which ran down a hill and crushed the tents of Midian, breaking them down completely and destroying them (de Granada, p. 24). The prophet Elisha improved the food of the disciples by throwing a little flour in the pot. The food turned sweet immediately. "So whoever wants to find remedy to the difficulties, disappointments and sorrows of this miserable life let him mix with them a little of this flour, let him approach this table and he will find in it enough sweetness to make his problems tasty" (de Granada, p. 24). Thus by receiving the Eucharist one can fulfill the proverb: "If one eats well one can better face daily problems because they seem to be less bitter" (de Granada, p. 24).

God communicates with us through the means of bread and wine because

it was a certain food which caused the ruin of the whole world and so decided that another one should be the universal remedy. . . . All this is not without a marvellous convenience or correspondence because just as our fall began with Adam . . . so also He wanted a second Adam to be the cause of salvation of the world as proof of His great holiness and justice. This has to be imparted to us through our union and contact with the flesh and blood of Christ who is in this sacrament. A figure of this can be read in the gospel, i.e., that the sick who had faith were healed when they touched Christ. Thus we are taught that by means of this spiritual contact with Christ we share in His grace, just as by the union of our souls with the flesh of Adam we share in his guilt. (de Granada, p. 25)

This sermon by Luis de Granada is a representative example of the many sermons on Corpus Christi which have been preserved. My comments should suffice to show the close relationship between the *autos* and the sermons. The topics developed, the arguments used, the examples from mythology, the parallels established between the Old Testament and the dispensations of the new law are indeed the same as those we continually encounter in the *autos*. To this I must add the identity of purpose: moving the will of the audience to a greater devotion and dedication to God.

## II  *The Eucharist and Silverwork*

In the Corpus procession the sacrament was carried in a monstrance through cities and villages. The monstrance was the central focus of this public religious pageant, and it was therefore only natural that this receptacle be appropriate for its purpose. It was usually made of the noblest materials. Ada Johnson says that "the highest refinement and development of this vessel belong to the fifteenth and following centuries."[7] The monstrances reflect the art of the period, that is, Renaissance silver work, which was greatly influenced in its turn by Renaissance architecture. The great art historian Camón Aznar stated that "monstrances are the most important contribution of Renaissance silverwork."[8] These vessels were not only exquisite works of art; they were, in some cases, full-length treatises on the Eucharist by means of images, statues, and inscriptions. The close relationship between this type of art and the *autos* can be seen clearly in the description we have of one of the most outstanding masterpieces: the monstrance of the cathedral of

Seville. The description was written by the silversmith himself, the famous Juan de Arphe y Villafañe, and published in Seville in 1587.[9] It was probably based on the instructions given to him by the cleric, Francisco Pacheco (Arphe, pp. 6–7).

The monstrance is several feet tall. It has four levels each shorter than the lower one. Each level rests on twenty-four columns: twelve large and twelve small (Arphe, p. 8). The first level consists of vines and children holding ears of wheat, "meaning bread and wine" (Arphe, p. 9). In the middle sits Faith and under her feet there is a globe of the world. Behind her there is a chained monster which represents Heresy (Arphe, p. 9). To one side there is a young man representing Intellect, as a captive of Faith. Opposite Faith there is a beautiful lady representing Human Knowledge and recognizing the majesty of the Catholic Faith. On each side of Faith sit St. Peter and St. Paul, with the Holy Spirit above them (Arphe, p. 9). Around the base are the four doctors of the Latin church, plus representations of St. Thomas Aquinas and Pope Urban IV. In the six niches are representations of the six sacraments (Arphe, p. 10). Since the sacrament of the Eucharist is the most important one, it occupies a more relevant place. Around each of the twelve pedestals there are three small scenes (thirty-six in all), eighteen from the Old Testament. The other eighteen are their counterparts from the New Testament and the history of the Church (Arphe, p. 11), for instance, the supper of the Paschal Lamb has as its counterpart the Last Supper of Christ. The description of this part of the monstrance ends with this observation: "Because all the sacraments receive their power and efficacy from the passion of our Lord and Redeemer, which is always commemorated in this most holy sacrament," several angels are placed on top of the columns carrying the different instruments of his Passion (Arphe, p. 17). In the pendentives of the arches there are several hieroglyphics and emblems with their mottoes all referring to some aspect of the Eucharist (Arphe, p. 19).

The second level of the monstrance is the most important one, for in its center the consecrated Host is carried. Around this space there are the symbols of the four Evangelists, and on the outside, the figures of the most famous local saints. In the six pedestals of this level there are six stories of as many sacrifices from the Old Testament, "which signified this most holy sacrifice of the Eucharist, so that one can see how this one is the culmination and the fulfillment of all the other sacrifices, and also that with its light the shadows of the others disappeared" (Arphe, p. 20). In the finials of these columns there are twelve figures representing the gifts of this most holy sacrament, as they appear in St. Thomas's treatise on this mystery. The six hieroglyphics of the second level are: a bunch of grapes, a hand with the index finger pointing to a chalice and a host, the rainbow with a chalice and a host over it, two crossed flashes of lighting with an olive branch in the middle, a pelican feeding its chicks, and a dead lion from whose mouth a swarm of bees is emerging (Arphe, pp. 21–24).

The third and fourth levels deal with the Church triumphant. In the third one we find the history of the Lamb, sitting on a throne, surrounded by four animals full of eyes, as indicated in Revelation. On the six pedestals there are many scenes related to the happiness of the blessed in heaven. All of them have eucharistic motifs, the most important being the banquet of the blessed in heaven. Under the arches of this level there are six hieroglyphics with their mottoes: a phoenix, two cornucopias full of vines and wheat, a kingfisher over its young chicks on a nest of vines and wheat, a carriage aflame going toward heaven, two dolphins holding between them a chalice with the Host, and an altar decorated with garlands of vines and wheat (Arphe, pp. 25–27). On the fourth level we have the Holy Trinity over the rainbow with many rays of light. On the fifth, there is a bell topped by a cross. Almost all the figures in the monstrance have one or more words clarifying the meaning. The vessel is one of great complexity and richness, but also of impressive clarity of design. It is an extraordinary example of magnificent Renaissance art created for the service of religion. The collaboration of a theologian and a great silversmith resulted in a masterpiece which has the Eucharist as its central theme. Many years would pass before a work of comparable richness and beauty would be created for the stage.

The use of allegorical figures, the parallelisms established between persons and events of the Old and New Testaments, the list of prefigurations and antecedents of Christ's sacrifice, the preeminence of the Eucharist, its presentation as the perfect synthesis and the central point of the history of salvation are all elements which appear consistently in the *autos*. These similarities point to a common source of information: the theological treatises and the devotional writings on the Eucharist. Monstrances and *autos* have an identical purpose: they pay homage to the Eucharist by moving the will of the spectator to a deeper and greater devotion of this mystery.[10]

### III  *Eucharistic Poetry*

Towards the end of the fifteenth century the Eucharist became the subject of many poetic compositions. The authors were mainly well-educated clerics, associated with the spirituality favored by Queen Isabella. Ambrosio Montesino (d. ca. 1512) was her preacher and Iñigo de Mendoza (1424?–1508?) was one of her favorite poets. Both were Franciscan friars. Hernando de Talavera (1428–1507), her confessor, a professor at Salamanca and a man of great religious zeal, had strong sympathies for Franciscan spirituality. He sometimes substituted parts of the liturgy with popular religious poems, and "he used to stage some religious shows so devout that only those who were harder than rocks could not help crying out of religious fervor."[11] The Carthusian Juan de Padilla (1468–1522) was one of the great imitators of Dante. All these writers treated the eucharistic theme with great precision of concepts and ideas. The poetic value of their compositions varied considerably. Their primary concern was to move the readers to religious fervor rather than to aesthetic rapture.

Marcel Bataillon grouped the poems of Montesino under two headings. The "religious songs" were compositions written for popular well-known tunes.[12] Under "devotional poetry" he included longer doctrinal poems, usually in five-line stanzas, intended more for private reading and meditation.[13] Montesino's *Treatise on The Most Blessed Sacrament (Tractado del Santísimo Sacramento)*, written for the Duchess María Pimentel,[14] has 656 lines. After a dedicatory preface and an invocation asking God's help, the treatise proper begins with four stanzas in praise of Faith, then proceeds to discuss the Eucharist as the memorial of Christ's passion and death, and as a token of eternal life. The Eucharist is the remedy to Adam's mouthful. In the Host the prefigurations of the Old Testament have found their fulfillment: the sacrificial Lamb, the showbread (Exod. 25:30), the manna. Mention is made of the Last Supper, especially the impact it had on the Apostles who, on being told what was happening, "did not bother to look for reasons which would clarify the mystery, but they washed their hearts with lamentations and prayers fitting the occasion. Some lost their senses, others changed their colors, still others started crying with intense sobs, seized by deep fears."[15]

The poem then explains the consequences of receiving the Eucharist worthily or unworthily. The sense of hearing is praised, for it perceives the precepts of Faith directly, and it cannot be deceived by appearances like the other senses. There follows a series of recommendations on how to worship the host, and the reasons why we cannot see God in it. The poet explains that it was the love and the great power of Christ which were the cause of this sacrament, and that we should be grateful for it. The poem ends with an apology to the Duchess for the shortcomings of the composition: the subject is sublime; before it his intelligence falters, and so he promises "to keep his tongue and his miserly rhymes under control."

The poem, then, is a rather long but well-sustained composition. The person to whom it was dedicated rather than the subject treated seems to exclude any lyrical outbursts or the popular treatment which is present in the later "religious songs" of Montesino and Mendoza. These poets were very much at home in the tradition of the Franciscan spirit. Their poems were simple and lyrical. To this tradition belongs Montesino's work "to be sung during Mass in honor of the sacred host," from which come the following excerpts:

Let not my senses give up before such a sublime mystery. Let not my thinking give up before such a sublime sacrament, but let my intellect soar up to it and nestle on it as if it were its nest. Natural reason, oh living bread, is unable to decipher you, but faith can fly up to you so that we believe that you are God. Let the heart rejoice because at the moment of consecration the Giver becomes the Gift by reason of His boundless love. . . . Because of this bread of heaven, which is a memorial of your passion, I will not give up my hope of receiving the crown of victory. . . . This new sweetness is much better than Eve's fruit, especially to those who eat it with sorrowful and repentant hearts. . . . [Spanish text] "No desmaye mi sentido / De secreto tan subido. / En tan alto Sacramento / No desmaye el pensamiento, / Mas vuele el entendimiento / Y en él haga su nido. / Cuanto natural escuela, / Vivo Pan no te revela, / La fe por alto te vuela, / Porque seas Dios creído / Regálese el corazón, / Que en esta consagración / El dador se torna don / Por amor muy desmedido / . . . Ya por este Pan de gloria, / Que es de tu pasión memoria, / De corona de victoria, / Pecador, no me despido. / . . . Es esta dulzura nueva / Mejor que el frutal de Eva, / mayormente a quien la prueba / Lloroso y arrepentido. . . .[16]

The following poem by Damián de Vegas, a dialogue between two shepherds, shows great similarity in language and tone to many passages in different *loas*[17] and *autos*:

Hey, Pascual, could you tell me what that white thing is over there? ¶ *Yes, Toribio, it looks like a wafer, but faith says that it is God.* ¶ How can such a great God fit into such a small thing? ¶ Toribio, faith teaches it. God knows how it is possible, Don't ask me such questions, for it is enough if I believe in it. *Toribio, it looks like a wafer, but faith says that it is God.* And it even says more: namely, that it is the remedy against Adam's poison. The outside looks like bread, but the inside is divine flesh. And if you ask me how all this is possible: *Toribio, it looks like a wafer, but faith says that it is God.* Toribio, one has to believe this, because it is useless to try to understand it; and God certainly knows how to do more things than we can understand. Toribio, what do you say about all this? ¶ I believe, Pascual, that that is the way things are ¶ *Toribio, it looks like a wafer, but faith says that it is God.*
[Spanish text] Pascual, no me diréis vos / Aquello branco qué sea? / ¶ *Toribio, parece obrea, / Mas dice la fe que es Dios.* / Cómo Dios tan grande cabe / En cuantidad tan pequeña? / ¶ Toribio, le fe lo enseña; / El cómo Dios se lo sabe. / Eso no me pidáis vos, / Pues bástame que lo crea. / *Toribio, parece obrea, / Mas dice la fe que es Dios.* / Dice más: que es medicina / Contra el tósigo de Adán; / De fuera parece pan, / De

dentro es carne divina. / Y si me preguntáis vos / Esto en qué
manera sea, / *Toribio, parece obrea,* / *Mas dice la fe que es*
*Dios.* / Toribio, hase de creer, / que entendello es por demás, /
Pues bien sabrá hacer Dios más / Que nosotros entender./
Toribio ¿qué decis vos? ¶ Creo, Pascual, que así sea /
¶ *Toribio, parece obrea,* / *Mas dice la fe que es Dios.*[18]

These examples should suffice for our purpose. The number
of authors and compositions was considerable. In them the
Eucharist is always treated with the seriousness and precision
which it demands. The poems showed great variety in language
and metrical forms, and some were exquisite literary compositions. A number of them were originally secular songs now
given a religious character through subtle changes in vocabulary.[19] The relationship of this poetry with the sacramental plays
in their early stages has not yet been satisfactorily explained.
Both seem to owe their origins to very similar motives and purposes. Many of the poems preceded the *autos,* but I cannot say
that they had a direct influence on the playwrights, even though
at a later period many of these compositions found their way
into the plays. In Valdivielso's *Romancero Espiritual* (1612)
there are many compositions which also appear in his *autos.*
Though the question of direct influence is still problematic,
the similarities between poetry and the plays is obvious. The
topics treated, the language used, and the dialogue form of many
poems show a tremendous affinity between both genres.[20]

### IV   *The Eucharist in Other Writings*

To conclude the present chapter, mention should be made of
the important place which the Eucharist had in the instructional
and devotional writings of the late fifteenth and sixteenth centuries. Many of the catechisms present a rather complete exposition of the doctrine of the Eucharist; they explain its double
character as sacrifice and sacrament, they see in it the fulfillment
of the prophecies and prefigurations of the Old Testament, and
the token of our eternal life. [21] A matter of continued controversy
is the frequency with which the sacrament should be received.
Erasmus's low regard for ecclesiastical ceremonies was interpreted by some as including Holy Communion, even though he

was very specific in advising its frequent reception.[22] Ignatius Loyola, Luis de Granada, Juan de Avila, and Ponce de la Fuente all advocated receiving communion frequently,[23] while others were noticeably more strict.[24] Catechisms and devotional treatises on the Eucharist increased considerably after the Council of Trent (1545–1563). A study of these works properly belongs to the history of Spanish spirituality. But an awareness of their existence helps us to better comprehend the familiarity of contemporary spectators with eucharistic doctrines, ideas and terminology which may be rather foreign to us today.

CHAPTER 3

# The Previous Dramatic Tradition

## I  The Medieval Beginnings

BEFORE we turn to the study of the *auto* proper, a few observations about the medieval Spanish theater are necessary.
The paucity of preserved dramatic texts has divided scholars
into two groups: those who practically deny the existence of
any significant drama, and those who see in the few extant
documents a witness to a very important dramatic activity.[1] The
first Latin play still in existence, the eleventh century *Quem
quaeritis* from Ripoll in eastern Spain, and the first play in the
vernacular, the *Auto de los Reyes Magos* ( ca. 1150), are considerably advanced in dramatic technique; they also show a
marked independence from the gospel passages from which
they were originally derived. They seem to point to the existence
of a tradition in which both liturgical and secular elements are
equally important. In a recent article, J. M. Regueiro concluded
that the religious and secular dramatic traditions "contributed,
though at different levels and importance, to the development
of medieval theater: the religious tradition contributed the
ritual frame, while the secular . . . brought the 'representational'
elements such as agile and fast moving dialogues within a lively
and clear scenic development."[2] The fusion of ritual material
with its three parts, pathos, peripety, and theophany,[3] and the
secular elements enriching its dramatic possibilities will be a
constant factor in the development of drama.[4]

For reasons political and literary, eastern and western Spain
developed different traditions. The eastern regions followed
European drama more closely. Though there was never anything comparable to the French miracle or mystery plays of
the thirteenth century, one sees in Gerona, Barcelona, and Valencia, a century later, the appearance of certain spectacles in

51

the procession of Corpus. They are directly related to the miracle plays.[5] Parker says that they were probably nothing more than "processional tableaux or pageants,"[6] but they were sumptuous and complicated productions, with intricate machinery, many dances, and choral groups.[7] In 1517 the characters actually recited a mystery, 278 verses long, called *El Paradís Terrenal*. We know that there were others.[8] Associated though they are with the feast of Corpus, these plays never dramatized any eucharistic theme. They remained basically medieval mystery plays, never developing in the direction of the *autos*.[9]

In the western regions, the theater associated with Corpus Christi went in a different direction. Recently discovered documents tell us that in 1445, during the Corpus procession at Toledo, there were some "spectacles" (*juegos*) which were probably no more than "simple shows."[10] Those of 1456, however, were "undoubtedly staged *autos*," but not yet the eucharistic type.[11] The famous writer Alfonso Martínez, in charge of the Corpus celebrations in Toledo from 1454 to 1457, had been in Barcelona in 1428 and lived in Valencia for ten years prior to 1450. It is possible that the plays at Toledo owed much to the ones in Barcelona and Valencia. In the following years, dramatic activity increased considerably in Toledo. In 1493 there were no fewer than seven plays presented, and similar activity continued in subsequent years.[12] In Seville, mention is made of a "float" (*roca* or *paso*) in the procession of 1454, the year of the first documented procession there. But no play is mentioned. The reason no doubt was the fact that plays were still being performed inside the cathedral. These plays "appear to have centered on the new feast of Corpus Christi."[13] Only in 1579 do these plays leave the cathedral to be performed in the streets and squares. "Here we have the Spanish *Auto Sacramental* as a development of the liturgical drama without the intermediate form of the miracle play evolved from a 'pageant'."[14]

A similar line of development seems to obtain in other southern cities such as Córdoba and Málaga, where in 1574 they were moved to the porch.[15] In the northern cities the situation is more varied. In Valladolid, plays were part of the procession before 1504, yet in Segovia a play was still performed inside the cathedral in 1598.[16] Parker assumes that these plays "may have been at least rudimentary *autos* since the method of their production foreshadows the future procedure at Madrid."[17] Parker's explanations of the origins of the *auto,* seemingly followed by Wardropper (Wardropper, p. 58), have been questioned by Flecniakoska (p. 270), and by Lázaro Carreter. Flecniakoska says that the *auto* "does not develop from any previous genre" (p. 270). Lázaro Carreter does not believe that "it is a development of the Medieval liturgical drama, but merely its chronological successor, without any genetic dependence from it."[18]

I believe that the sacramental plays in their technical aspect as drama depend on the previous tradition. Their originality consists in their content and more specifically in the new point of view from which this content is presented. The liturgical theater and the mystery plays concentrate on one biblical event or on a series of them. They follow the original story rather closely. The relationship of the stories presented to the culminating fact in the history of salvation which is Christ or the Eucharist could be said to be more implicit than explicit in the text. The sacramental play, on the other hand, has at its very center the eucharistic mystery, from which every moment of the history of salvation receives its meaning. The similarity in content and point of view between the *autos* and Catholic Liturgy is very close. The sacramental plays can therefore be called liturgical drama of a special kind. They are not only in honor of the Eucharist; they are about the Eucharist. They are not really concerned with dramatizing the historical institution of the Eucharist but rather its meaning as the central point in the mystery of salvation.

The date this important step was taken remains a matter of controversy. Cotarelo y Mori proposed the *Sacramental Play* (*Farsa Sacramental*), probably written before 1520 by Fernán López de Yanguas, as the first *auto.*[19] Parker called such a suggestion absurd, adding: "The *Auto* Sacramental was no new genre that suddenly sprang up to life, but the gradual fusion of separate dramatic traditions, and it is impossible to point to this fusion as being first exemplified in any one particular play."[20] I do not think Cotarelo's and Parker's opinions are mutually exclusive. We know that the first Corpus plays were liturgical or mystery plays. At a certain moment the Eucharist became the main subject of the plays. This new development would create a new dramatic genre, although in its origins it was totally dependent on the previous tradition. The decisive factor here is the presence of the eucharistic theme in the text of the play as the essential element. It is not enough that the play be performed in a eucharistic context, i.e., on Corpus day, as Lázaro Carreter had suggested for the plays performed in Spain's eastern cities, [21] and as V. A. Kolve had offered also for a similar situation in England.[22] The eucharistic theme has to be an essential part of the play.

Attention should be turned now to the dramatic materials and techniques which the authors of the *autos* found at their disposal and of which they readily availed themselves. I will commence with the *Coplas de Mingo Revulgo* (ca. 1465), and the *Coplas de Vita Christi* (1482) by Fr. Iñigo de Mendoza, so closely studied by C. Stern.[23] The former is a dialogue between two shepherds satirizing the lamentable political situation and suggesting possible remedies. The poem, which follows the mode of pastoral allegory, became tremendously popular, and traces of its influence can be found in many works. It contributed considerably to the frequent use of pastoral allegory in early Spanish drama, including the *auto,* and to the language used in similar works. "The die was cast then, with the *Coplas,* and the Sayagués became the linguistic medium for the stage shepherd for the next two hundred years."[24] Mendoza's work was also very popular. In the first part of the poem one finds what Stern calls the Nativity play. Although, as she says, "there is by no means any unanimity concerning its dramatic nature,"[25] she thinks that there are two simultaneous scenes present: the shepherds' dialogue and the adoration by the angels, each on a different stage. Stern concluded "that the inspiration for the early part of Mendoza's narrative poem was in fact actually a lyrical and dramatic celebration that the poet himself witnessed each Christmas season in Spanish churches."[26]

In this work and subsequent ones of the sixteenth century, Stern detected an "indebtedness to medieval folk festivals."[27] Thus, for instance, the lyrical direction given to the early literary drama was the inevitable consequence of its development out of medieval dance-songs in which spoken dialogue is virtually non-existent."[28] She concluded: "The literary drama, which appears at the end of the fifteenth century, has deep roots in medieval folk tradition. The lack of medieval dramatic texts should not deceive us, therefore, into assuming that the drama was unknown in medieval Spain. . . ."[29] Equally important for the future *auto* is the dramatic activity represented by the *coloquios* in Seville [30] and the plays, already mentioned, staged at Toledo from 1493 to 1510.[31] One can see this rich tradition of anonymous plays surfacing again and taking final form in the *Códice de Autos Viejos*.

## II  *Gómez Manrique, Encina, Fernández, Vicente*

With Gómez Manrique (1412–1490?) begins a series of playwrights who give the theater a more learned tone and dramatic tightness. Manrique's works were few and simple, but in a sense they prepared the way for Juan del Encina (1468–1529).[32] Encina's first works owed much to the medieval mysteries, while his later plays looked definitely to the Renaissance. The former ones have more interest for us. In them one usually finds a very appealing set of shepherds who speak the language and react very much like their real counterparts. There is a symbolic dimension in the names of some of the shepherds; also there is a curious desire to explain the meaning of the festivity in terms of the history of salvation; finally, generous use of musical elements provides great dramatic value.[33] Of particular significance is the use of the fulfillment of prophecies as a dynamic element in the action. In later authors the emphasis will be on prefiguration. Nonetheless, both elements have a similar dramatic value, that is, to move the heart through a devout understanding to an explosion of worshipping joy, which can only be adequately expressed in lyrical song. The plays usually follow this outline: presentation of an extraordinary event; explanation of the event as the fulfillment of prophecies and promises by God; and last, boundless rejoicing and thanksgiving. The use of the fulfillment of the prophecies and of the elements of prefiguration for their probatory value is common in the New Testament. Christ himself used them on his way to Emmaus (Luke 24:13–35). In the *autos* they become an important dramatic element for they are used as the arguments which move the protagonists to the desired conclusions, thus advancing the action to a joyous ending.

Lucas Fernández (1474–1542), a writer of secular and religious plays who had much closer ties to the feast of Corpus than Encina, took part in the Corpus celebrations at Salamanca in 1501, during which some of his own plays (*juegos*) were staged.[34] Two years later his "play of the shepherds" was presented,[35] and in 1505 he was busy again in the preparations for the feast.[36] Fernández was a great composer. Music is more important in his plays than in those of Encina. His *Dialogue for Singing* (*Diálogo para Cantar*) "is a little opera,"[37] a possible predecessor of Calderón's musical plays. In Encina's *Third Eclogue* (*Egloga Tercera* 1493 or 1494) one finds an old hermit dialoguing with a young one. Now in Fernández's *Eclogue or Play of the Nativity of Our Redeemer Jesus Christ* (*Egloga o Farsa del Nascimiento de Nuestro Redemptor, Jesu Christo,* 1500) it is a learned hermit who explains Christ's incarnation to the shepherds. The same thing happens in his *Play of the Nativity* (*Auto del Nascimiento*). The angels who instruct the shepherds have been replaced here by a hermit or, in other plays, by a monk or a shepherd;[38] later on it will be by Faith. An interesting detail is the fact that, among the arguments of prefiguration which Fernández used to show the truth of the incarnation, he mentions the brazen serpent, Noah's Ark, the Paschal Lamb, and Isaac, all of which usually appear in relation to Christ's passion and death, and the Eucharist.[39]

In the *Play of the Passion* (*Auto de la Pasión,* before 1503), his masterpiece, we find the first reference to the Eucharist in any Spanish play (Wardropper, 170–71). The songs at the end of the play have a very eucharistic tone. The first one "gives to the play a certain air of a sacramental play, since it refers to the monument toward which the characters are walking (processionally?) as the tabernacle where our sacramental life is kept."[40] This procession is an old ceremony dating back to the Mozarabic liturgy. [41]

Gil Vicente (1475?–1536) knew Fernández personally and

was well acquainted with his works and those of Encina.[42] His *Play of St. Martin* (*El Auto de Sant' Martinho*) was staged in a church in Lisbon for the Corpus of 1504, but lacks eucharistic character. In his plays, following Encina and Fernández, Vicente replaces the Christmas angel first with a hermit and then with a shepherd, for instance in *The Castilian Pastoral Play* (*Auto Pastoril Castellano*, 1502) and in *The Play of the Magi* (*Auto dos Reis Magos*, 1503). Of greater interest are two of his other works: *The Play of the Sibyl Cassandra* (*Auto da Sibilla Cassandra*) and *The Play of Faith* (*Auto da Fe*). The first one is a good example of how anachronistic elements can be used successfully to illustrate the topic dramatized. The joint appearance of Abraham, Moses, Solomon, and the four sibyls is justified by their intimate relation to the mystery of the incarnation. Deliberate anachronism of this kind will be a constant phenomenon in the *autos*. In *The Play of Faith*, the main character, Faith, explains to two shepherds the feast of the Nativity. (Faith will be one of the most common characters in the *autos*.) Besides these two important plays, Vicente wrote several morality plays in Portuguese where he shows a perfect mastery of the allegorical technique. These works also help to prepare the way for the *autos* to come.[43] Vicente's morality plays contributed greatly to the success of the dramatic allegory in Spain. But allegorical works were also written by eminent humanists who most certainly helped the future playwrights. The following observations seem to me to be pertinent here.

Everything seems to indicate that the first authors of *autos* were ecclesiastics associated with university life. The Spanish universities, from the end of the fifteenth century on, were the principal focus of religious and cultural reform. Andrés calls the years 1500–1530 "The Period of Cisneros."[44] In every respect they were years of unusual optimism. The universities of Salamanca and Alcalá enthusiastically took on the renovation of all learning. The humanists advocated and practiced a return to the sources, but at the same time they created important works of their own. This double aspect of their activity can be seen in respect to allegorical works. Aurelius Prudentius's (348–415) great allegorical poem *Psychomachia* was reedited with a commentary by Nebrija in 1512, 1536, 1540, and 1546.[45] In 1522

Alvar Gómez published the poem *Thalichristia*, 16,400 hexameters long, in which, according to Nebrija, "he succeeded in harmonizing theology and poetry in the most beautiful way possible."[46] The poem deals with all the important theological topics, beginning with the mystery of the Trinity and ending with the final conversion of the world. In 1529 Francisco Palomino published his Spanish translation of Prudentius's *Psychomachia* with the title *The Battle or Struggle of the Soul (Batalla o Pelea del Anima)* which was reedited in 1559.[47] Between 1563 and 1572 Father Acevedo wrote a play in Latin entitled *The Battle Between the Virtues and the Vices (Bellum Virtutum et Vitiorum)*.[48]

These notes should suffice to help us evaluate the favorable climate provided for the emergence of the *auto*, through a deep appreciation of the allegorical mode. The Eucharist was also the theme of theological works. I will limit myself to mentioning Nebrija's commentary on the eucharistic hymn "Pange Lingua," which is really a treatise on the Eucharist as mystery, sacrifice, and sacrament. The commentary was part of his *Aurea Hymnorum Expositio*, published in 1522 and reedited almost thirty times. [49] The various questions dealt with in this chapter should give an adequate idea of the literary and religious situation in Spain at the beginning of the sixteenth century when the first *autos* appear. As dramatic works they profited from the attainments of the previous tradition, with its religious and secular elements, a language both learned and popular, a series of realistic and allegorical characters, and a great appreciation for the dramatic value of music and song. Finally, as religious and allegorical works, the *autos* found two great allies in the impetus of ecclesiastical reform and in the writings of the humanists.

CHAPTER 4

# The Early Autos

## I  *The Sacramental Play of López de Yanguas*

FERNÁN López de Yanguas (ca. 1487–ca. 1545) was a hu-
manist who taught in several cities. All of his works have
a clear didactic bent.[1] His *Triumphs of Madness* (*Triunfos de
Locura*) is an allegorical work, an Erasmian satire of practically
all social classes. *Questions* or *Problems* (*Preguntas* o *Problemas*)
is also allegorical, with Desire and Rest as protagonists. Up to
the present only four of his plays have survived, one in very poor
condition, and it is precisely the one considered to be the first
*auto*, which I will presently analyze. The *Eclogue of the Nativity* (*Egloga de la Natividad*) has a very simple structure,
similar to the early ones of Encina, but there are a few erudite
references to mythological figures. Christ is presented not only
as the fulfillment of prophecies, but also as the one directing
and performing many of the outstanding deeds in the Old
Testament (vv. 121–28, 145, 336, 343). Christ's birth appears,
then, as the final theopany in a long series of minor ones. His
actions have a supratemporal dimension, and that is why in
him facts separated by centuries find unity. It is explained that
Christ was in on everything, before his final revelation as God-
made-man. For instance he was the one who turned Aaron's
rod into a serpent, who saved the children from the fiery fur-
nace, who stopped the sun in the middle of the sky, and who
tamed the lions in Daniel's den, etc. The character Gil Pata
cannot understand how the newborn baby could have done all
that "more than a thousand years ago" (v. 182). Mingo Sabido
answers that it is because He now "begins to be a man, but He
is and was God who made the heavens and the world" (vv.
191–92). Christ's genealogy is given with great detail, and
there is a faint allusion to his future redemptive work. He will

59

conquer evil, and his sheep will be marked with a red brand, and "the wayward ones will be brought back to His fold where they will find sacred and blooming pastures" (vv. 302-3).

*The Play of the World and Moral Play (Farsa del Mundo y Moral*, 1524) is a clumsy piece of two quite different and independent parts. The first part, of interest here, is a good didactic piece showing how Faith can help Appetite to be set free from the World with the help of a Hermit who represents "preaching and religion" (v. 33). This allegorical debate portrays in miniature an interior conflict of conscience. It is presented in such a way that we can see the psychological process of a moral choice. The outline of such a process is classic in its simplicity. It is in this part that "we find certain typical characters of the sacramental plays" as Wardropper observes (p. 181). The conflict of the moral choice is in essence the same that will appear countless times in the *autos*: the choice between God and the Devil.[2]

Yanguas's *Play of the Agreement (Farsa de la Concordia*, 1529) was written to celebrate the Treaty of Cambray of the same year between France and Spain. It is an allegory whose protagonists are Mail, Time, World, Peace, Justice, War, Rest, and Joy. The work of this author of greatest interest here is the *Sacramental Play (Farsa Sacramental)*. No date can be given, though González Ollé thinks it must be prior to 1521.[3] The original text has been lost. Only a few verses remain, together with the summaries of the action prepared by Cotarelo.[4] Four shepherds, Jerome, Ambrose, Gregory, and Augustin, are puzzled by certain extraordinary phenomena in the skies and on earth which they cannot understand. An angel comes, "the same who came this year to our fold" (v. 18), probably meaning the angel of the Nativity plays. The reason for such portents (he says) is the feast being celebrated today, Corpus Christi, when Christ gives himself to us as food. Gregory inquires how this can be, and the angel explains with a long list of biblical texts. They finally accept it as fact, and in a kind of Creed they confess that Christ was "the one who did this or that thing, always using passages from the Old and New Testaments."[5] A series of songs follows in honor of the sacrament. Suddenly Ambrose asks "how is the heavenly Jerusalem we are hoping for?" The

angel describes it according to Revelation. The play ends with
the shepherds returning to their folds, singing several songs.

The structure of the play is very similar to that of the Nativity
plays. The great novelty is the theme and the way it is presented.
The Eucharist becomes a synthesis of the history of salvation.
The angel, using a long series of texts from the Bible, explains
the Eucharist to Gregory. Cotarelo's summary is not explicit,
but I would guess that these texts are the types and prefigurations of the Eucharist in the Old Testament. For the shepherds,
these texts are an adequate proof of the truth of the mystery
being celebrated. Scenes similar to this one are very important
for the dynamics of the *autos*. The result of such proofs is always
a genuine and profound act of faith and adoration on the part
of the characters. Among the final songs is the "Tantum Ergo,"
probably sung by the audience as well. The Eucharist already
appears in this *auto* in its most universal dimension: Christ is
present in it. Since Christ is one with the Father and the Holy
Spirit, they are also present in the Eucharist (vv. 31–32), which
thus contains the fullness of the divine life. The Eucharist is
the fulfillment and the realization of past promises. For us it
also marks the beginning of our life with God which will have
its total expression in the heavenly Jerusalem described in verses
43–50. The joy of this thought makes the four shepherds sing
and dance a hymn of thanksgiving.

Cotarelo called this piece the first sacramental play. A. A.
Parker strongly opposed him on this. Wardropper agrees with
Parker giving as a reason the lack of allegory, though "we can
find in it, in embrionic form, some of the elements which charac-
terize the Calderonian *auto*" (p.179). In addition, there is no
question that "the symbolism of the [shepherds'] names opens
the door to the allegory to come." More recently, González
Ollé considers the play a genuine *auto*, not only because it has
a eucharistic theme, but because there is in the play a certain
type of allegory, for "the central theme is dealt with in a way
which is technically very close to allegory."[6]

The controversy clarifies the fact that the play is a borderline
case which naturally presents certain difficulties of classification
common to most early manifestations of a new literary genre.
The play is not, in fact, an allegory, but follows the structure

of the Nativity plays; however, the doctrinal aspect of the eucharistic theme is identical to that of the more advanced *autos*. The
Eucharist, the sign par excellence of all God's actions, is given
to us as food, the nourishment of the new life here on earth;
and it is a prophetic sign of life in the heavenly Jerusalem. The
play presents in simple outline what the Liturgy does on a
grander scale. In the Mass, through readings and instructions
we are led to acts of worship and thanksgiving. The play wants
to move the will of the spectators to greater devotion through
similar means. In the *Farsa*, four different liturgical songs are
mentioned. One of the protagonists commences singing them,
but I am inclined to believe that they were meant to be sung
by the audience as well, thus underlining the play's character
as an important part of the worship of the day.

## II  *The* Play of the Most Blessed Sacrament *(1521)*

Since no sure date can be assigned to Yanguas' *Sacramental
Play*, we cannot say categorically that the anonymous *Play of
the Most Blessed Sacrament (Farsa del Santísimo Sacramento,
1521)* is a development of the former, as is generally admitted.
The similarity between the two works is considerable. Cotarelo
in fact thought that both could belong to Yanguas. After examining all the pertinent information, González Ollé prefers to
consider it anonymous.[7] For Wardropper, "the identity of the
author is not important. What is more noteworthy, from the
point of view of the *autos*, is the fact that this play has gone a
further step away from the Christmas plays and moved in the
direction of the eucharistic plays" (p. 180). The great innova-
tion is the appearance of Faith explaining the doctrine of the
Eucharist. Faith, to be sure, was already a character in Vicente's *Play of Faith* (1510). It is mentioned three times in the
Liturgy of Corpus, and is constantly present in the devotional
poetry and religious literature of the period. But this is the first
time that Faith appears in a play about the Eucharist.

The piece, with the same basic structure as Yanguas's *Sacramental Play*, lacks dramatic action, but is rich in doctrinal
content.[8] The story deals with three shepherds, two of whom
have seen and heard some extraordinary manifestations of joy

in the sky and on earth. A young man appears to Justino and says that these phenomena are because of today's feast, telling him to go and join the celebrations in the villages. Thus, he and the other shepherds can offer Christ "their life, their souls, and their hearts" (st. 15). Pelayo, the ignorant one, asks for further explanations, and Justino replies that only Faith can give them. She appears, "richly dressed . . . young and beautiful" (st. 17). She knows what the joy is all about. Pascual and Justino hope she will explain since "she knows everything . . . even things that Greece ignored and Rome could not understand. She can impart the secrets that she saw and learned to persons of all kinds" (st. 18). The ignorant Pelayo finally adopts the right disposition, asking Faith to explain this important feast, and Faith readily agrees to do so. The author has set the stage for the exposition that follows by having the characters open themselves up to the supernatural. Pelayo, the ignorant or faithless one, has not seen the heavenly manifestations. Justino and Pascual have. Their acceptance of the supernatural can be made clearer by Faith alone. She will not attempt to *prove* anything, only to illuminate and put in sharper focus what they already believe. Her way is not the way of pure reason: neither Greece nor Rome could ever know what she knows.

The long section that follows is an alternating mixture of expressions of boundless joy motivated by doctrinal and devotional considerations that situate today's feast in the context of the history of salvation. Attention is centered continually on the concrete and specific feast being celebrated. The words "today," "today's feast," or "this feast" are repeated many times. But their meaning is varied, for they refer simultaneously to the moment of the institution of the Eucharist at the Last Supper, to the celebration of Corpus Christi in 1521, and of course, to any celebration of the Mass. The peculiar unity of the history of salvation is thus brought out very clearly. "Today's celebration" recalls and commemorates the main stages of this history which are made present here in a special way and which are mentioned in no particular order.

Christ in the Eucharist is the same eternal Word begotten by God (22b), who comes from God (24, 36b, 76a). He is God made man (19f, 21f, 22h), God who created every thing, includ-

ing man, from nothing (29, 54a) and who sends angels to men
for their protection (26cd). He came from God, He is again
with Him, seated at His right hand (42d, 47d). He was born
of the Virgin at Bethlehem (30gh, 36c, 38fg, 53ef), He suffered
and died on the cross (10ef, 37f, 39d, 47e, 54f, 56h, 74cd). His
death and the Eucharist are presented as intimately united, for
the Eucharist is a memorial of His redemptive work (53gh,
54cd) for all of us (19h). The eucharistic bread is the same that
was sown inside the virginal sacred womb (37bc), the same
that was born at Bethlehem and drank the milk of Our Lady
(38fg). He is the same who received, in the body now present
(the Host), the wounds and the lashes which shocked everyone. Through his death he freed us (39); he is the same bread
which was baked with the fire of love on the cross (37ef, 54f).

The sacrament was instituted at the Last Supper when Christ
was the priest and the sacrifice at the same time (49g). After
having eaten the ritual Lamb, he decided to take away the
shadows and let the true sun shine, thereby opening the gates
of heaven for everyone (45). The true meaning of the Old
Testament is thus revealed: it was a preparation for the mystery
of Christ. The author explains this further with a beautiful
comparison worth quoting in full:

> As a painter, wishing to  paint a panel starts by drawing on
> it the appropriate lines, adding later on the final colors, so also
> our Redeemer, at the table (of the Last Supper), begins to draw
> the outline with the (eating of the) Lamb, and then finishes,
> with (the offering of) His own Body, this most valuable paint-
> ing".
> [Spanish text] "Ansí como suele hazer el pintor / al tiempo que
> quiere la tabla pintar, / que con ciertas rayas la suel señalar, /
> después acaballa con vero color, / ansina en la mesa nuestro
> Redentor / comienza con el cordero a rayar, / y con el su cuerpo
> nos quiso acabar / aquesta pintura de tanto valor" (st. 46).

The Eucharist is thus put in a very special relationship with
many events of the Old Testament. Adam sinned, but Christ's
sacrifice will erase it (53cd, 56, 69ab). The Eucharist was fore-
shadowed in the manna (35), the bread and wine offered by
Melchizedek (40ab), and the utterances of the prophet David

(40ef, 50cd) and Samson (50f). Several portents of the Old Testament are adduced as proof of God's power: the rivers being turned to blood, the conversion of the rod into a serpent and again into a rod (31), Elisha's iron floating on the water, and Joshua stopping the sun (32). Thus it is easy to accept the conversion of bread and wine into His body and blood (31, 32). The powers of death and evil have been neutralized and destroyed (27e, 61). The attitude of the individual Christian toward the Eucharist becomes the decisive factor of his ultimate fate. Judas, the greedy ones, the sinners and evildoers, the blasphemers, and all who receive it unworthily will be condemned (48, 49, 63, 64, 65).

For those who have been cleansed from Original Sin in baptism and from personal sins in the sacrament of penance (56, 62), the Eucharist becomes a source of continuous joy, of which the present celebration is an example. God's actions give human nature a new dignity (27a, 57cd). He even gives men the power to change bread and wine into His body and blood (41fg). Pilgrims that we are, Christ has become our redeemer, our helper (58, 59, 76b). Man's only possible answer is a grateful and total dedication to Christ, indeed to the Trinity also present in the Eucharist (36). Christ's Redemption marks the beginning of the last period in the history of salvation. Christ, present in the sacrament, gives man true hope and life (59ab); it becomes a token of man's future life with Him (59gh) for it has the power to take us to His glory (10gh, 55h, 68gh), the heavenly Jerusalem (70, 71, 72), Mount Horeb (76d), and heaven itself (76g). No wonder then that this should be a day of rejoicing for all (9eg, 15e, 19e).

The *Play of the Most Blessed Sacrament* is a rich collection of eucharistic motifs. However, it lacks the coherence and tightness of good drama. Its message is one of joy, and the play gives many reasons which justify that joy. Later authors would return again and again to the same material and use it with better dramatic effect. The work, then, has little dramatic merit. The possibilities for dramatizing Pelayo's passage from ignorance to consent are neglected in favor of the exposition of the meaning of the feast. References are made to the fate of those who receive the Sacrament unworthily, but they are not developed dramatically. The accent is definitely on the joy of the celebration. The play is very close in tone and content to the sequence of the Mass of Corpus Christi.

### III  Diego Sánchez de Badajoz (1479?–1549)

Modern critics are very much in agreement about the importance of Sánchez in the development of the *auto*. His work is indeed of the utmost interest, not so much in terms of masterpieces achieved but in terms of the possibilities he created for future writers of *autos*. Immediately after the title of his *Collected Poetical Works* (*Recopilación en Metro*, 1554), he says that in it "many items ('figuras') and passages from Sacred Scripture are presented and explained in an entertaining, courtly and pastoral style."[9] In the introduction, his nephew wrote that the subjects of the book are "things taken from the very heart of Sacred Scripture." The style is "clear and tangible," it is not so dry or so dense that it may tire the ears with empty concepts. On the contrary, "it is witty but with discretion, it is well-planned carelessness, for [the author] was not only very erudite, but a man with great creative mind and very mature judgment."[10] A reading of his works immediately confirms these observations. Sánchez shows great familiarity with the Bible, with a marked tendency for surprising interpretations of familiar passages. For instance, King Solomon's decision regarding the fate of the baby brought to him is usually seen as an instance of his wisdom. In Sánchez's view, the bad mother represents the Synagogue, and the good one the Church. At still a higher level, the bad mother is the flesh; the good one, the soul. The baby in question is Christ himself.[11]

Sánchez's dramatic works are not easy to classify. Lopéz Prudencio grouped them as moralities, mysteries, and farces.[12] Wardropper prefers to call them pseudomysteries, pseudomoralities, and farces (p. 187), while Crawford divides the twenty-four works according to the occasions upon which they were probably staged: Christmas, Corpus, saints' feasts, and occasional pieces.[13] These divisions, however, fail to give us an idea of the contents or technique of the works. Among his Nativity plays, there are some which are basically allegorical. Some of the Corpus pieces, on the other hand, do not even mention the Eucharist. Generally, his Nativity plays are superior to those of Corpus. In some of the Nativity plays allegory is used very successfully, for instance in *The Moral Play* (*Farça Moral*) and *The Military Play* (*Farsa Militar*). Sánchez also uses allegory in nontheatrical works. The *Collected Poetical Works* opens with a poem entitled *Spiritual Hunt in which Reason Hunts Will, Followed by a Commentary with a More Detailed Interpretation.*

Reason goes out accompanied by a hunter (Judgment), two track dogs (Prudence and Justice), a bloodhound (Faith), a greyhound (Hope), and a wolfhound (Charity). They all go into the human mountain (v. 24), looking for Will. They find her and surround her "showing her signs of love" (v. 72). Reason, then, shoots an "arrow of love" (v. 76) "dipped in the blood of the Lamb" (vv. 80–81). "That brushwood of errors" (v. 98) opposes them, but finally Will surrenders. The first part of the poem has 128 lines, while the commentary or gloss has 480. In it we find a very detailed analysis of the struggle of the moral man, with Reason the winner. The poem is a well-sustained allegory. At the end of the title was added, "A deeply felt composition," and it was undoubtedly so. It was meant to be a very serious piece in which the profane and comic elements so prevalent in his other pieces are totally absent. The poem shows a vivid imagination capable of portraying psychological processes in very visual and dramatic terms.

Even more impressive for its dramatic force is the description of the struggle of conscience in the *Rational Play of Free Will* (*Farsa Racional del Libre Albedrío*) "in which is represented the battle which takes place between the spirit and the flesh. The protagonists are Free Will armed with all her weapons; the Body as a shepherd; the Soul as an angel, tied to him; sensuality as an evil woman; Carelessness as a shepherd; Understanding as a doctor; Reason as a queen."[14] Free Will, the perfect gallant, strong, resplendent, and very proud of himself, decides to marry. He encounters Body and Soul tied together very uncomfortably. Body offers Free Will their daughter, the most beautiful girl in town. They talk about the human condition after the Fall until Sensuality (Body's daughter) appears.

In a beautiful speech (vv. 388–415), she tries to seduce Free Will. The dialogue that follows is a very interesting portrayal of Free Will's inner debate. After rejecting Understanding's advice, he surrenders to Sensuality: "Oh what a great pleasure it is to enjoy your beauty! I put my freedom captive in your hands" (vv. 587–90). The repugnant presence of Carelessness, however, immediately makes him realize the truth of what he has done and the moral ugliness of his union with Sensuality. Soon the process of repentence begins, which ends in the marriage between Free Will and Reason (vv. 714–21). The scenes where the contrasts between appearance and reality are described anticipate similar ones in plays of the seventeenth century.

The present work has been unanimously praised as one of Sánchez's best. It is comparable to the *Spiritual Hunt*, mentioned above, in the ease with which the action moves, the perfect rhythm of the changes, and the truth of the sentiments described. This is indeed true drama with a tragic element vividly portrayed. The allegory here is very skillfully blended with the action. The text yields its meaning naturally, becoming ever clearer as the work progresses. A minimum of imagination is enough to see the theatrical interest of the play perfectly: the gallant but gullible man-about-town who ignores his fallible condition and the advice of his intelligence, only to fall in love with the wrong lady. But he does not lack the courage to repent and to finally marry his equal. The outline of the play could well be used for a secular piece. In it I find the true makings of excellent theater.

In the *Moral Play* (*Farça Moral*) and in the *Military Play* (*Farsa Dicha Militar*), there are similar scenes of beautiful allegory and deep psychological insights vividly dramatized. The same can be said about the *Dance of the Sins* (*Dança de los Pecados*). Many of Sánchez's allegorical characters are much more than vague abstractions. They posses strong individualistic traits which make them very alive and realistic. Sánchez's innate capacity for symbolism and allegory also appears in a number of short Corpus pieces written for the guilds. He can easily find interesting and moving relations between the tools of the trades and spiritual and religious realities by developing their symbolic possibilities. For instance, he establishes a close parallel between the cultivation of the wheat and the life of Christ in *The Play of the Beekeeper (Farsa del Colmenero)* (vv. 349–92), in such a way that "you can see very well how the Lord manifests Himself to you in your toil and sweat" (vv. 401–3). He describes the symbolism of the work of the bees and ends his commentary by saying: "I omit a thousand other lessons so as not to bore you; be satisfied with things like these which you can observe in your hives" (vv. 561–64). López Prudencio calls this work "a little sacramental play."

The dignity of the smithies is described in *The Play of the Blacksmith (Farsa del Herrero)* and in *The Introit of the Black-smiths (Yntroito de Herradores)*, where Sánchez spells out the symbolic dimension of some of their products. The horseshoes and the bridle are absolutely necessary for horses to do their work well for "a beast of burden without horseshoes and without bridle is useless" (vv. 34–35). As for man, the fear of God is like a bridle: it stops him from running after foolishness. The love of God, on the other hand, is like good horseshoes which enable us to tread the rocky path of this life (v. 79). In many of Sánchez's works one can see a perfect combination of the insights of the moralist with the sure technique of an excellent dramatist. Valdivielso and Calderón are later examples of the same phenomenon.

C. Sabor de Cortázar has studied in depth and detail the way Sánchez portrays the faculties of the soul and their reciprocal action. Her study makes obvious that, if some of his plays are perfect theater, their doctrinal content is perfect moral theology. For her the basic and most fundamental aspect of Sánchez's plays is "their didactic nature and the means used to impart their message."[15] The theater is for him a form of preaching, a means he cultivated with the utmost care. "What impresses us in these plays is the precision of his reasoning, the subtle logic, the inflexible scholastic discipline of mind of which he boasts."[16] Her analysis centers on two works: *The Spiritual Hunt* and *The Rational Play of Free Will*, but her conclusions are applicable to all others. She states that his ideas are not original, but the way Sánchez dramatizes them certainly is, for "he presents them operating together, in living reciprocity, in one single action. A rigorously articulated thought process succeeds in giving a panoramic view which makes it possible for one to understand the complex psychological workings. . . . This primitive and rustic theater shows itself, then, not as a naive means of entertainment, but as an example of surprising intellectual lucidity in the service of religious instruction."[17]

Another aspect worth our attention has been studied diligently by Flecniakoska. It has to do with Sánchez's preoccupation with the total theatrical success of his works. It can be evidenced in the many stage directions which he carefully supplied, specifying the type of dress, the accessories, and the stage movements of the characters. For Sánchez, "the play is not just a literary work, but the text of a dialogue placed within the spatio-temporal frame of an action, according to a given movement or rhythm."[18] Flecniakoska lists some sixty-five different utensils or accessories, sometimes used more than once. He tells us that the actions, gestures, and movements of the protagonists are often indicated, stating whether they should move fast, run, go slowly, or walk very proudly (*muy ufano*). The stage directions "show us how great was Sánchez's sense of the theater. . . The study of the exits and entrances of the different characters makes us realize that we are dealing with a theater in which rhythm and movement are always present."[19]

Another aspect of his art which deserves special mention here because of its importance in the history of the *auto* is his interest in biblical allegories as exemplified by the following plays Sánchez wrote for Corpus Christi: *The Play of Isaac* (*Farsa de Ysaac*), *The Play of Moses* (*Farsa de Moysén*), *The Play of King David* (*Farsa del Rey David*), and *The Play of Abraham* (*Farsa de Abraham*). These biblical allegories are of quite different quality. As dramatic works they are in general inferior to his other plays. In them the theologian and the preacher seem to have supplanted the dramatist. Their importance lies in the fact that prefiguration is used to a greater extent than ever before. In previous works, persons and events were mentioned for their prefigurative value, but now the entire work is a dramatization of one or another event, emphasizing the connection it has to the Eucharist. The results are not always satisfactory. The flow of the allegory is interrupted by doctrinal explanation deemed necessary by the playwright to make the lesson more explicit. This didactic emphasis can be seen clearly in the use Sánchez makes of the traditional shepherd introducing the play. He has some of the traits of the clown and trickster found with other authors, but he is also the one who explains the meaning of the work and who remains on stage to intervene with an elaborate explanation whenever necessary.[20]

A good example of Sánchez's biblical allegories is *The Play of Isaac*.[21] A shepherd greets the audience in a humorous way, calls for attention and explains what they are going to see: the story of Jacob stealing Isaac's blessing from his older brother Esau. In a surprising interpretation of this passage, Sánchez makes Jacob represent the Jews and Esau the Gentiles. The story has great value as a prefiguration of the Eucharist (vv. 44–45). The shepherd laments how easy it is to deceive our senses except for our hearing. This is followed by advice to keep the faith through sound hearing (vv. 53–60). With this warning the shepherd introduces one of the main themes of the *auto*: the preeminence of hearing in regard to the acceptance and conservation of faith. Sánchez has here in mind St. Paul's text: "Faith comes from hearing, and what is heard comes from the word of Christ" (Rom. 10:17). But the source of the shepherds ideas is most probably a stanza from St. Thomas Aquinas's hymn "Adorote devote," which says: "The senses of sight, touching and taste are deceived in you (the Eucharist) and one can safely believe only through hearing."[22]

Isaac, old and blind, sends Esau to hunt for something for him to eat. As Esau leaves, Rebekah tells Jacob to kill two kids to prepare for Isaac. In that way the father will give him his special blessing. The shepherd breaks in to criticize those who say they are unable to work but show themselves very willing to rob and steal. If he were in a position of authority he would beat them mercilessly (vv. 116–25). Jacob returns with the kids, and the shepherd makes good his threat, attempting to take them away, claiming they are his; he realizes just in time that they don't have his brand on them. Rebekah and Jacob leave, and the shepherd, alone on stage, criticizes some mothers' preference for one child over the others. Rebekah and Jacob return, and she dresses him with Esau's clothes. The shepherd breaks the action again to comment on how deceitful appearances can be. The food is ready, and with it comes a jar of wine which the shepherd greets happily.

The stage is set for the main experiment: the testing of the human senses. Jacob calls his father who answers: "I hear you well" (v. 207). Jacob comes before him, and Isaac thinks he is Esau. The shepherd observes that the sense of sight has been deceived (vv. 214, 216–17). Isaac touches Jacob and thinks he is Esau, which the shepherd duly comments upon as a failure of the sense of touch (v. 222). However Isaac knows that the voice is that of Jacob. The shepherd comments immediately that hearing has not failed (v. 225). Isaac eats the food, not realizing that they are his own kids, and the shepherd points out that taste has also deceived him (vv. 231–40). The meal over, Isaac kisses Jacob and compares his smell to that of a rich field, allowing the shepherd to observe that smell has also failed him. Finally it is time for the lesson. The shepherd had warned the audience about the great mystery prefigured here (vv. 49–50). So now, taking center stage, he goes directly into the interpretation, applying what has happened to the Eucharist, whose substance is God but has the appearance of bread (vv. 251–52). We should not try to investigate this secret because the senses deceive us, and the only sure way is that of faith which comes from hearing (vv. 256–60). We should use our hearing to accept what he said: "This is my body." If anyone has doubts, faith will satisfy them. These are God's great miracles, and only he can perform them.

And now he pauses to tell the audience to listen to Isaac's blessing. He asks God to give Jacob an abundance of bread, wine, and oil. The shepherd observes that with oil the soul is purified, and in the bread and wine God gives us His divine body and blood (vv. 281–85). When the blessing is over, Esau comes and learns what has happened. The shepherd intervenes several times to comment on Esau's sad situation. Isaac then blesses Esau: he will be rich in the fruits of the earth but will have to serve his brother until the time comes when he will be free from this yoke (vv. 359–60). The shepherd seizes upon this to explain that this time has already come: Jacob will not be master to Esau anymore. After Christ's coming, he who behaves better, is better. We all eat from one divine bread and drink from one chalice, for now we have God with us, who made one thing of both. The play closes with a song in which all are invited to rejoice because God has called us all, and he has blessings for all of us.

Whatever the play's weaknesses, we must recognize Sánchez's merit in having attempted to present a biblical story in an allegorical way. Future authors would have greater success, but he initiated the trend. Allegory as a method of literary interpretation goes back to prechristian times. Greek and Latin authors saw the need to explain some of the stories in Homer, Hesiod, and Virgil in terms of a meaning above and beyond the literal one. One thing was said, but another understood.[23] Influenced by Greek thought, some Jews in Alexandria began interpreting the scriptures looking for a spiritual meaning beyond the literal one. Philo of Alexandria (30 B.C.—A.D. 45) is the best representative of this school. His exposition of the Pentateuch is an excellent example of this type of exegesis.[24] With the advent of Christianity, biblical interpretation was given a very specific goal and direction. Christ himself compares events in his life with those of the Old Testament. In his Gospel, Matthew puts particular emphasis on presenting Christ as the fulfillment of prophecies. For St. Paul, many of the Old Testament stories are allegories or prefigurations of the realities of the New. The early Fathers of the Church attempted to systematize the allegorical interpretation of the Bible.

It was again in Alexandria that Origen (185–254), heir to the Greek and Jewish tradition, developed a method of interpretation with three different levels: the literal, the moral, and the anagogical.[25] His influence on later commentators was enormous. However, his low regard for the literal meaning made his approach not totally acceptable. The Fathers of the West sought to correct it by giving the literal meaning its proper dimension, that is, its historical value, without diminishing its prefigural character. St. Augustine and later on the Scholastic writers developed a more comprehensive figural system of interpretation according to which persons, events, and objects of the Old Testament, without losing their historical character, were types, prefigurations, shadows, and first drafts of persons, events, and objects of the New. The latter ones in turn are types and pre-figurations of the final realities in the heavenly Jerusalem.

In this way a series of relationships obtains which ignores and is above the strict chronological order of things. The pre-figurations of the Eucharist, for example the bread and wine offered by Melchizedek (Gen. 14:18), the Paschal Lamb (Exod. 12:1–14), the manna (Exod. 16:13–21) or the bread and wine mentioned in Isaac's blessing do not have any real connection, historically speaking. And yet they posses a unity by being anti-cipations of the Eucharist where their meaning is fulfilled and completed. From this particular perspective the dramatists can legitimately bring together elements which, though separated by centuries, have among themselves profound relationships. They are ultimately based on the fact that the first ones are prefigurations and the last ones the fulfillment of one and the same reality. This method of interpreting the Bible is not an arbitrary one, for it is ultimately willed by God himself. The interpreter's task is to discover its workings.[26] Because it is more demanding and restricted, it never succeeded in supplant-ing the more personal and freer form used by Origen. Many of the spiritual and mystical writers of the Middle Ages fol-lowed in this tradition, their writings at times degenerating into a sort of subjective and unbridled panallegorism.[27] The authors of the *autos* avail themselves of one or the other method, depending on the nature of the work they are writing. The poetic character of their compositions allows for a freer inter-pretation of biblical texts than in more serious theological com-mentaries of the Bible.

In the preceding observations I have commented on biblical allegory as a method of interpretation. Sánchez, however, uses it to create dramatic works. If he did not succeed completely, it was precisely because he treated the stories more as an interpreter than a dramatist. *The Play of Isaac* fails because the allegorical interpretation of the two parts—the test of Isaac's senses and the meaning of his blessings—have neither been given tight cohesion nor integrated into the action. The unity of the play is thus to be found in the original story, but not in the allegorical interpretations, where one should expect it. The didactic intention has prevailed over the exigencies of drama.

The lessons are clearly drawn: the primacy of hearing in matters of faith, the prefigurative and prophetic value of both blessings, and especially the presentation of the Eucharist as the synthesis and fulfillment of both Testaments. The freedom promised to Esau was achieved by Christ who communicates it to us through the elements mentioned in Jacob's blessing. Thus Christ made both Testaments one (v. 370). Biblical allegory will succeed only later on when the stories proper assume a secondary place in the works, namely that of illustrating the allegory.[28]

In the preface to the *Collected Poetical Works,* Sánchez's nephew mentioned the fact that the book is humorous, "witty but with discretion, it is well-planned carelessness" (pp. 49–50). This is indeed one of the striking aspects of his style. A similar mixture of the sacred, the profane and the humorous could be somewhat disconcerting if one were not familiar with the long tradition that preceded Sánchez.[29] The purpose of these comic scenes is made clear by Sánchez when he says in the prologue to *The Play of the Nativity (Farsa de la Natividad):*

"There will be devout and useful things, but to prevent you from falling asleep we will say a few things which will make you laugh." [Spanish text] "Serán cosas / deuotas y prouecho-sas, / y porque no vos durmáys / algunas cosas graciosas / diremos con que riáys" (vv. 124–28).

As W. Shaffer Jack has pointed out, Sánchez's comic episodes belong to a period of transition where the relationship between the humorous parts and the main play sometimes does not exist or on the contrary can be very strong.[30] An example of the first case is the second half of *The Theological Play (Farsa Teologal).* Similar scenes would soon find a rich life as separate plays known as *entremeses (interludes).* A good illustration of the second can be found in *The Play of the Miller (Farsa del Moli-nero)* where the appearance of the picaresque blind beggar serves to stress the lesson which the friar has been giving the miller: the blind man's guide is to him what faith is to the believer, for "regarding the sublime mysteries, faith is the one to guide us and to lead us to the mountain of eternal life along smooth paths" (vv. 301–4). In cases like this, the comic element is quite effective both as entertainment and as a demonstration of very important truths.

The preceding remarks should give an adequate idea of Sánchez's contribution to the development of the *auto*. Besides his poetical works, he also wrote a book of sermons and a manual for penance (Sánchez, p. 47). The theater was probably one of the most congenial ways he found to discharge his catechetical duties, and he used it very skillfully. The historian of the sacramental plays, however, cannot help having mixed feelings towards him. For while he deserves high praise for his abstract allegories, he also missed great possibilities in his eucharistic plays. Sánchez shows deep familiarity with the allegorical method of interpreting the Bible, but he never arrived at a satisfactory integration of this method with the demands of good theater. Sánchez's excellent abstract allegories, probably inspired by Prudentius's *Psychomachia*, and depicting in dramatic terms the inner struggles of the moral man, would serve future authors well. They could easily convert them into *autos* by introducing the eucharistic theme. On the other hand, with his experiments in biblical allegory, Sánchez opened up a new avenue of possibilities which other playwrights would cultivate more successfully. His facility to relate everyday objects and ordinary occupations, by means of their symbolism, to higher spiritual realities gave a very concrete, almost tangible character to spiritual truths. His allegories are thus very effective, both dramatically and pedagogically.

## IV    *The* Códice de Autos Viejos (*1550–1575*)

From the very personal art of Sánchez de Badajoz I pass now to a series of anonymous plays. Some of them have only been published recently, while others are still in manuscript form. All of them, however, are in need of much critical study. The first collection, the *Codex of Old Plays*, (*Códice de Autos Viejos*), contains ninety-six works which were written from 1550 to 1575, according to their modern editor.[31] Almost all the works are anonymous, and all but one have a religious subject. One third or fewer deal with the Eucharist in such a way that one can call them sacramental plays. Most of the others present stories from the Old Testament and other devotional themes. Many of the latter ones were very probably performed at Corpus. The collection, then, contains a rich panorama of the religious theater of those years. This was a transitional period out of which the *auto* would emerge much more clearly defined. The terminology was still very fluctuating. The word *auto* referred not only to pseudomysteries but also to sacramental plays. The phrase *farsa del sacramento* meant that the play could have some eucharistic motif but was not allegorical, while *farsa sacramental* indicated a eucharistic theme in allegorical form (Wardropper, pp. 226–28).

The topics of the plays vary and resist classification. Wardropper probably offers the best one (pp. 220–21):

| I. Pseudo mysteries | 1. Biblical themes |
| | 2. Hagiographic themes |
| II. Intermediate type suggested by Sorrento | 1. Adam themes |
| | 2. Resurrection themes |
| III. Pseudo moralities | 1. Allegorical autos, non-eucharistic |
| | 2. Allegorical plays, eucharistic |

On the basis of the amount of allegory present in the plays, Wardropper suggests the following division: I. Plays entirely allegorical; II. Plays predominantly allegorical; III. Semiallegorical plays; IV. Plays slightly allegorical. Wardropper's classifications are preferable to those of F. Wolf, L. Rouanet, L. Sorrento, and A. Valbuena Prat, and they help the reader understand the variety of works in the collection and different stages of artistic development. A trait common to practically all of these works is the almost exclusive use of the five-line, eight-syllable strophe (*quintilla*).

The *Códice* is thus a rich miscellaneous collection of plays, written by different authors representing varied local traditions. It is very possible that the texts preserved are not the original plays but rather later revisions. At least such is the case of *The Play of the Accusation Against Humankind (Auto de la*

*Acusación Contra el Género Humano)* which is the revised
Spanish version of the Catalan miracle play, *Mascarón*, dating
from the fourteenth century.[32] The importance of the *Códice*
for the history of the *auto* rests on the significant number of
eucharistic works that it contains and on the considerable artistic level reached by some of them; also, on the variety of
topics to which the authors resort to present the Eucharist.
There are several Old Testament stories whose eucharistic dimension is very skillfully brought out and developed, for instance *The Sacrifice of Abraham (El Sacrificio de Abraham)*,
*The Play of the Manna (Aucto del Magna)*, *Joseph's Wedding
(Los Desposorios de Josef)*, and *The Bride of the Song of Songs
(La Esposa de los Cantares)*. From the New Testament come
*The Fountain of Grace (La Fuente de la Gracia)* and *The Play
of the Sacrament of the Evangelists (Farsa del Sacramento de
los Evangelistas)*. Contemporary civil and religious conditions
in Spain are used in these *autos*: *The Tribunal of the Church
(Las Cortes de la Iglesia)*, *The Sacramental Play of Peralforja
(Farsa del Sacramento de Peralforja)*, and *The Marriage of
Spain (Las Bodas de España)*. On the other hand, *The Play of
the Child Intellect (Farsa del Entendimiento Niño)* has a rather
abstract content.

One can see how the range of topics used to present the
Eucharist has increased. Old Testament stories will be used
more and more frequently, and medieval mystery plays will be
transformed into beautiful *autos*.[33] Contemporary conditions are
dramatized to illustrate some aspect of the Eucharist. In these
plays are reflected some of the serious problems which ecclesiastical and civil authorities had to face, especially the large
number of Moorish and Jewish converts and the Protestant
menace. Moors and Jews appear in many plays as one of the
more crucial concerns of many playwrights. But in terms of
possible topics, the Old Testament will remain one of the most
important sources, at least in part due to the intensive studies
of the Bible and of the writings of the Fathers of the Church
enthusiastically promoted at the universities.

At this point I will analyze three plays which in my opinion
represent an important advance in the development of the *auto*.
The first is *The Play of the Manna*.[34] The introduction (*loa*)

warns the less intelligent in the audience to be extremely attentive and to use all their powers of discrimination before they pass judgment on the play. As for the others, he tells them that "I will deal as best I can with the greatest favor that the Lord of Heaven has given you. I will deal with the food into which God transubstantiated Himself" (vv. 11–17). A few lines later he says that the play will deal with the manna, a very special prefiguration of this bread and a sure means of transforming us into God. The introduction ends with this last warning: "All of you keep wide awake and beg God with great faith that what I am going to say does not fall into arid hearts" (vv. 21–30). The play proper dramatizes the story found in Exodus, chapter 16, verses 4–36. Some very important changes have been made in order to make it good theater. For instance, instead of the anonymous mass of the Israelites of the original story, the author has singled out a few of them and has given them sharp individualizing traits. In the Biblical passage there is practically no dialogue, while here of necessity everything is dialogue, alive and fast-moving.

In the first part of the play, Reuben and Manasseh complain bitterly about the critical situation, while a peasant underlines the same ideas with comic observations, lamenting the total lack of bread. In the second nucleus, Lia and Rudilia, carrying their hungry children, join in the complaints. The scene is very effective, dramatically speaking. Bread is mentioned three times as the possible remedy for their intense hunger. In the third nucleus Moses and Aaron promise them God's intervention. The two leave to intercede with the Almighty, while the others continue to complain. In the last nucleus, Moses and Aaron return, followed immediately by an angel who gives them bread—God's bread sent from heaven. The play ends with a eucharistic song addressed to the Blessed Sacrament, the true bread of heaven, present in the monstrance during the representation of the play.

In his brief analysis of this piece, Wardropper does not mention the all-important introduction. He calls the play a pseudomystery, denies that it is allegorical, and says that the last song "is nothing more than a lyrical summary of the meaning of the drama"(Wardropper, p. 225). The play however is a biblical allegory. A better understanding will be arrived at

if one is able to reconstruct the staging of the play, paying
special attention to its three movements. The introduction is of
the utmost importance here, being an essential part of the play
which provides the key to a correct understanding of the story
as a prefiguration of the Eucharist. The warnings of the introduction definitely preclude a literal understanding of the original
story. The second movement is the play proper. The outline of
the biblical story has been maintained, but changes have been
made to achieve a dual purpose: a dramatic nature is given by
reducing the number of characters and by giving them a sharper
individuality; and second, a clearer eucharistic interpretation is
made possible by identifying the manna as bread and describing
it in terms commonly used for the Eucharist. The last movement
is the final song. The three stanzas begin with the words "this
bread," referring to the Host present in the monstrance. Words
and gestures underline the value of the play as a biblical allegory of the Eucharist. Having said this, I must hasten to add
that the play by itself, that is, if one excludes the introduction
and the monstrance with the Host, is perhaps not a complete
dramatic unit. On the other hand, it seems obvious to me that the
author saw all these elements as one single unit and that we
should try to understand it accordingly.[35]

The second play I would like to analyze briefly is *The Bride
of the Song of Songs* (*La Esposa de los Cantares*).[36] The title
refers to the biblical poem, *The Song of Songs*. The main protagonists are Christ and the Soul, not as lovers but as marriage
partners. The play is a good example of excellent unfulfilled
dramatic possibilities. The introduction (*loa*) recommends joy
this day. Christ offers himself as food on the divine table, to
which he invites Humankind. To make this invitation more
forceful, Christ decides to marry Humankind. The play proper
opens with Grace recommending confession to those who want
to reach the glory where God inhabits. The invitation is to any
"humble sinner." Body and Soul appear and hear Grace's invitation. Body would like to accept; it is an invitation to eat, any-
way, and he has not eaten at all for some time. But Grace
rejects them, because, despite having been married to Christ
spiritually, Soul has abandoned Him for a villain, the Devil.
Soul knows this is true. Grace undresses Soul, a graphic way of

indicating her loss of spiritual grace, telling Soul that, if she wants to return to her husband's presence, she should ask for Confession, Contrition, and Penance, who will tell her about Him. Body and Soul blame each other for yielding to that "black ruffian." the Devil. Finally, both agree on their mutual guilt, and Soul says: "Let us look for my Husband and my God with tears of bitterness" (vv. 132–33). Soul turns to the audience with a moving plea: "Have they seen, perhaps, her love of loves . . . the best-looking man among all creatures? He is white, blond and ruddy-faced. His face is radiant and He is altogether comely" (vv. 140–46).

Confession, Contrition, and Penance enter next. They know her Husband well. Body and Soul repent; they will soon be washed with the soap of penance. Body leaves the stage; he is to be disciplined with a whip. Soul remains alone. After a fervent prayer to her Husband to come and show her His face, Christ appears, saying: "How are you, my dove, my wife and my sweet love?" Soul dares not come close but He tells her encouragingly, "Oh my dearly beloved spouse, welcome! Tell me, are you very tired?" She answers: "Oh radiant face of yours! . . . Give me your sacred hand, because I am so weak and suffering, so hungry and thirsty, that I am about to fall, fainting." Christ responds: "I will give you to eat of my sacred flesh, transubstantiated into bread. And you will drink my blood, shed for you" (vv. 260–88). Suddenly Soul asks Him why He offered Himself on the altar. He answers that Melchizedek prefigured this bread of consolation. The Father ordained Him a priest in heaven. In the Last Supper He prepared the sacrifice and He finished His holy Mass on the cross. In that supper He took bread and wine and transubstantiated them. He remained in the sacrament and at the same time returned to the right hand of the Father.

Soul asks who can understand that. He could explain it, He says, but it would not be good for her. It is better to believe it on faith. Soul agrees. He tells her to stay and once her journey is over she will enjoy Him. "And if you are attacked, just call me and I will come to you" (vv. 321–22). And he says goodbye with an embrace. Hypocrisy appears as a sly go-between, telling Soul that a handsome man is very hurt by her behavior.[37]

His name is Mr. Satan. Soul reacts violently. Satan himself appears and Soul rejects him with equal strength. She implores Christ, who comes instantly to help her, and He repeats that she will soon see Him at the end of her journey. Body returns dressed in clean clothes given him by Grace, surrounded by Contrition, Confession, and Penance. Body and Soul rejoice. The last scene represents the end of the journey for Body and Soul. Fortitude appears, sent by God to take them with her for "the time has come to enjoy what was promised" (vv. 453–54). Body of course wants to know whether they will be given nourishment. Fortitude answers: "Here God Himself is the food." Body is happy and the play ends.

The defects and imperfections of this piece are all too obvious. However, I think it is more important to look at the possibilities it suggests for other plays to develop. The Eucharist is the most important element of the play and incidents of the story are directly related to it: Man's fortunes vary according to his attitude toward the sacrament. Important also is the portrayal of the relationship between Christ and Soul and Body, as that of partners in marriage. The idea is found in several biblical texts, and spiritual and mystical writers have also used it frequently. Then, too, the influence of the secular theater cannot be overlooked here. The rivalry of the two lovers for the lady, the services of the go-between, and the scene of Souls' seduction are details which indicate the author's capacity to borrow from different sources in order to present religious material with new originality.[38] The sacramental plays and the secular theater frequently benefited from each other. The mutual contacts would increase in number and significance as the sixteenth century drew to a close.

The third play I wish to analyze is *The Play of the Triumph of the Sacrament (Farsa del Triunfo del Sacramento)*.[39] It opens with Pride trying to console Envy who is crying bitterly. Her suffering is so intense, she says, that "if the heart wants to express what I feel, pain shackles my tongue in the middle of the explanation" (vv. 20–24). She finally manages to give the reason: "Know, then, to your astonishment, that our eternal God has created an animal whom everyone calls man" (vv. 45–48). God has placed such an unworthy thing made of dirt, above His angels. Pride promises to snare him. She would like to destroy the universe and return it to its primeval chaos. She remembers how she defied God and was followed by legions of angels. Now they will plot to make man sin, so that State of Innocence, who lives in Paradise, can be put in Death's jail, oppressed with heavy chains.[40] Pride and Envy send reluctant Sin and Deceit to capture State of Innocence who comes on the stage dressed as fool, happy in the abundance of Paradise. He had a dream: Sin and a beast had attacked his parents, and both fell and soiled themselves. He leaves the stage to find out if this is true.

Deceit returns triumphant, and Pride promises him Lust for a wife. He captured State of Innocence with the help of Gluttony and that of an excellent relative called Appearance of Good and False Hypocrisy. State of Innocence now enters with Sin riding on his back. He feels lonely in a foreign land and would like to have something to eat, but all they offer him is work and suffering. Death is called in to put more chains on State of Innocence. He cries but to no avail. His name will now be changed to Original Sin. To compound his misery, Death climbs on Sin and Sin on him, and so he has to carry both until they reach Death's prison. Pride and Envy leave to celebrate the wedding between Deceit and Lust.

There is now a complete change on stage. Disobedience (Adam) and Human Fragility (Eve) complain about their lost glory and their present sorrow, arguing about whose fault it was. They wander around looking for help, and knock at the door of Divine Goodness, asking for forgiveness, but it is Divine Justice who answers. She calls herself Avenging Justice and will not help them. They proceed and knock at the houses of Mercy, Reason, Charity, and Faith, but Justice is always the one who answers them. Finally they reach Hope's door. Hope gives them a promising answer: "God will change your sorrows into Joy by rescuing your sons" (vv. 752–54). God will become man and give His life for them. She will let them know when this is going to happen. They leave, filled with hope.

The stage changes again. Mercy wants Justice to accompany her and liberate State of Innocence. Justice agrees as she considers herself well paid now by Christ's sacrifice. Faith agrees but, as a condition for the return of the redeemed son, states that his parents must believe with firm conviction a mystery never heard of before. The mystery is that "on this happy earth, and under that veil, under the appearance of bread, our God is contained, and that He is here on earth, the same as He is in heaven" (vv. 820–24). They bring the good news to Disobedience and Fragility. Faith explains what Christ has done and asks them to realize that "if you became ill by eating, you will be well again by eating too" (vv. 858–60). Disobedience asks how God can be in heaven and in the host. Faith gives two examples: the flavor and aroma which remain in every part of a divided apple and the image of a person reflected in every piece of a broken mirror. Disobedience is totally satisfied, "and since God can do anything He wants because of His power and His infinite knowledge, I don't want to investigate any longer how He can do it" (vv. 950–54). Now Justice frees Original Sin, who is not too happy to see his mother again. But she tells him that this is not a day for complaints because our Lord "as a token of what is to come in the next life, decided to remain here in order to console us" (vv. 992–94). The new realities force another change of name: Original Sin will be known as State of Grace. Sin, Pride, and Envy are captured and chained, and they will remain so, since we can dominate them all "with the help of the sacrament" (v. 1034). The play ends with a joyous song.

This piece must be ranked among the best in this collection. It is a perfect allegory, well controlled at all times. The intense language, the excellent characterization, the variety of scenery, and the easy flow of the action all contribute to a deeply satisfying aesthetic emotion. Reading it, one cannot help comparing it with those *autos* by Calderón, such as *Life Is a Dream*, in which the history of the redemption is presented with such a sweeping view that it never fails to impress the reader.[41]

J.–L. Flecniakoska rightly says that the *auto* survived and developed because it knew how to make good use of the advances in secular theater.[42] Some of the plays analyzed here show an obvious desire to borrow plots and situations that could well serve the eucharistic purpose. The ultimate conflict of moral life, the choice between good and evil, can be expressed in many dramatic ways by resorting to the many forms which good and evil can assume. It is true that in the sacramental plays and from a theological point of view "there would be no drama without Satan's presence, for he is at the very source of all conflicts."[43] But he can take many different shapes, as many as all the evil temptations to which our sensual and intellectual appetites are subject. Our playwrights understood this very well, and at times they succeeded in giving it excellent dramatic form.[44]

## V  *The Plays of Manuscript 14.864 (1575–1590)*

In this section, the plays to be analyzed are found in a recently published manuscript, dated 1590.[45] Probably written between 1575 and 1590, of the eleven anonymous plays only six are *autos*. The works, as drama, do not represent an improvement over those of the previous collection. Wardropper thinks that among them "we find sacramental plays more developed than any written by the authors of the *Códice*" (Wardropper, pp. 236–37). In my opinion, however, they cannot be compared, for example, in dramatic power and control of form to *The Play of the Triumph of the Sacrament*. Their main contribution is to be found in their daring experimentation with secular literary topics for a eucharistic purpose. I do not mean the borrowing of small details or references to mythology, contemporary literary, or political facts, but rather the adoption of a complete secular structure which, through subtle changes, is transformed into an allegory with a new religious content.

Let me examine the most important ones beginning with *The Comedy which Deals With the Rescue of the Soul (Comedia que Trata del Rescate del Alma)*,[46] the second play of the collection. It is a religious rendering of an extremely popular legend in which the knight, Don Gayferos, brings the beautiful Melisendra back to freedom after her capture by the Moors.[47] This legend was the subject of many anonymous ballads. The popularity of these ballads among learned poets had been growing since the second half of the fifteenth century. Many of them found their way into the theater,[48] and religious poets accommodated them for religious purposes. The present *auto* belongs to this tradition. Its author also shows great familiarity with other literary sources which have been diligently identified by A. Kemp.

The outline of the play has certain similarities to *The Play of the Triumph of the Sacrament*. As it begins, Soul (Melisendra) is already suffering the consequences of Original Sin. The Devil keeps her chained in a dungeon. Soul's sad condition has lasted about five thousand years (the period from after Adam's Fall until the coming of Christ). She cries and begs God to remedy her situation; she has hope. In heaven, meanwhile, Christ (Don Gayferos) and Divine Love are about to play a game. If Divine Love wins, he will give everything to man. He does win and prepares to fulfill this promise. A curtain opens on one side of the stage. Father and Holy Spirit appear, and the former tells Christ that it is time to rescue His captive spouse. It will be a very costly rescue, for Christ Himself will be the ransom and the money, but He will be rewarded by being seated at God's round table.

Flesh tells the Devil the news, and they exhibit frantic panic. Soul has a dream: Hope comes to announce her rescue. Christ, made man, comes to meet Soul, and there is a beautiful scene of gallantry between them, similar to those scenes between suitors and lovers in secular plays (vv. 625–886). Christ's sufferings and passion are then alluded to. The Devil, the World, and the Flesh have been defeated, and the resurrected and triumphant Christ meets with Soul who is baptized and given the sacraments together with the final instructions. Christ is ready to return to heaven, but He decides to stay in the Sacrament, and Soul is deeply grateful.

The play presents in outline the main points of the history of salvation, and it does this very successfully. The sources used have been very skillfully adapted to the new ideas. The legend plays an excellent suggestive role embellishing the theological content, never obscuring it. The elaboration of the eucharistic ideas is perhaps somewhat wanting, limiting itself as it does to the final lines. The presence of some passages in prose leads Kemp to suggest the possibility that "the author did not complete his task of making a metrical version."[49] The lack of poetic elaboration that one feels in some scenes lends some support to this suggestion.

Another *auto, The Sacrament of the Eucharist (Sacramento de la Eucaristía)*, successfully presents the Eucharist as the central element in the life of the Christian man. Our final fate is determined by our attitude towards the Eucharist. St. Paul developed this doctrine in the second half of chapter eleven of his first letter to the Corinthians. This play seems to be its first dramatization in Spanish.[50] The unity of the play is broken by a rather long comic scene. This scene, independent and easily detachable, does not diminish the clarity of line and the structure of the rest of the play. The introductory song puts the sacrament in its proper cosmic setting, as fire, air, sea, heaven, and earth owe it reverance. For its part, man's reverence or the lack of it becomes the measure of his fate. Tiberius and Virtue accept the sacrament with all the consequences. Ambrose, though instructed by them, prefers the company of Idleness. Justice comes with a sword to carry out the sentence decreed in heaven to kill him "who sinned against the Sacred Lamb" (vv. 492–3) and Ambrose dies and goes to hell. Then an angel comes to crown Tiberius, thus anticipating the happiness of heaven where they will enjoy "a sweet, happy and joyous meal" (vv. 604–5). The last scene is a beautiful elaboration of the moral lesson of the play. The lyrical tone, the music, and the actions bring this out very forcefully. Calderón, in *Belshazzar's Banquet (La Cena de Baltasar)* would present as only he could one aspect of the same teaching: the fate of the sacrilegious or defiler of the sacrament. The doctrinal content is the same in both plays.

*St. Paul's Conversion (La Conversión de S. Pablo)* follows very closely the story as related in the Acts of the Apostles, chapter 9.[51] This fact plus the total absence of allegory would seem to put into question the play's nature as an *auto*. Buck holds that the eucharistic element is no more than an appendage to make the play conform to the spirit of the feast.[52] Wardropper, however, thinks that it deserves the title of *auto* because of the opening eucharistic song and the concluding invitation to partake of the Church's banquet (Wardropper, p. 238). His interpretation seems more acceptable. St. Paul gives us one of the

four accounts of the institution of the Eucharist (1 Cor.
11:17–34) and yet, Buck observes, "this *auto* is the only one of
the Saint Paul plays I have examined which introduces the
subject."[53] It is surprising that it took so long to make the connection. The reason is probably the considerable resistance to
a satisfactory blending of accurate historical facts with the
symbolic world of the sacraments. Besides the opening song
and the banquet at the end, two references are made to Paul's
hunger and thirst. They are worth quoting: "I feel so hungry
and so thirsty for the baptized people, that the blood already
shed is not enough to satisfy me" (vv. 61–64). Later on, Christ
entreats Ananias to take care of the newly converted Paul because "he has not eaten in three days" (v. 454). These allusions
could have been poetically elaborated, but they were not. Also,
the play always stays very close to historical facts. The experiment did not have any succesful imitators.

   *The Castle of Faith (El Castillo de la Fee)*[54] is a beautiful
allegorical piece. The castle of the title is not the soul, as in
several other plays, but, first, the body in which the soul lives,
and, second, Spain under attack by the Heretical Soldier. The
two levels of meaning are kept separate. The references to
historical conditions in Spain never interfere with or obscure
the more spiritual and universal meaning of the play. Preoccupation with heresy, specifically Protestant heresy, appears in
many *autos*, but, given the positive orientation of the *genre* as
a celebration rathen than a defense of the faith, the danger of
heresy is just one more possible spiritual hazard against which
the faithful are warned.[55] The struggle against heresy plays a
rather minor role in the history of the *auto*. A glaring exception
are Mira de Amescua's plays, as I will show later.

   *The Castle of Faith* deals ultimately with the inner workings
of the life of faith, the dangers to which it is exposed, and the
rewards which the spiritual man receives for his victorious
struggle. The allegory is very effective. Contemporaries were
very familiar with all the play's elements: Castles were still
strategic places of defense, and heresy was an obvious reality.
But the castle had been used as a metaphor of the soul by religious and mystical writers. In the castle (Body) lives beautiful
Soul. In the play, Faith is more than the custodian, it is the

firm foundation of the castle. Prayer is the sentinel, always on the lookout. Care has the keys and also keeps watch over Prayer, so that they do not fall asleep. When they eventually do, the Heretical Soldier enters. Faith wakens them, and they all seek and apprehend him, soon after which he decides to renounce his beliefs. When he does, they promise him the Eucharist.

Buck mentions "the serious tone of this *auto*, in which comedy is entirely lacking."[56] The play, a very positive and joyous statement on the importance of the life of prayer and vigilance, with the Eucharist as the token of the ultimate reward in heaven, offers an impressive dramatization of some of the doctrines found in many contemporary treatises on prayer and the spiritual life, meant here for the benefit of a larger audience. *The Castle of Faith* is a good example of the way in which abstract or literary allegory, as opposed to biblical allegory, began to be used in order to dramatize the moral content of the eucharistic doctrines. As a technique of literary creation, allegory had had a long and successful history going back to the story of Plato's cave in the seventh book of his *Republic*. In Christian times, Prudentius (348–415) wrote the poem *Psychomachia* to describe the soul's moral struggle between good and evil. His influence was to be great and lasting.[57] Boethius's (480–524) partly allegorical *De Consolatione Philosophiae*, Capella's *De Nuptiis Philologiae et Mercurii* (ca. 500), and other poems gave allegory a prestige which it was never to lose. Medieval Spanish literature is rich in allegorical works of considerable beauty.[58] Later spiritual and mystical writers made frequent use of it. Medieval morality plays adapted the technique to the exigencies of the theater, bringing it to a high degree of perfection.[59] In the sacramental plays it found a new and impressive manifestation.

Allegory, as I mentioned before, says one thing and means another. An allegorical work has, then, at least two levels of meaning. First of all, it tells a story in concrete, human, perhaps historical terms. *The Castle of Faith* can be read as the story of an assault on a castle. Fletcher insists on this aspect when he says that "the whole point of allegory is that it does not need to be read exegetically; it often has a literal level that makes good enough sense all by itself."[60] The success of the work depends to a great extent on how interesting the story is at this level. However, for the total meaning of the work, this level is of secondary importance. The author wants the work to be understood at a higher, more abstract, and therefore more universal level of meaning. He will achieve this by giving the reader a series of hints which will indicate his intentions adequately. Some are very subtle; others are very obvious. In this play, the title itself indicates the metaphorical nature of the castle. In many others, the title does not provide such a clue. The same can be said about the characters in the plays who may appear from the beginning as abstract ideas or may become the representation of such ideas as the play develops.

Since the first literal meaning of the story assumes a secondary importance, it does not always have the coherence and fullness that it would if it were told independent of the allegorical context. The world as a theater is a valid metaphor, but Calderón, in *The Great Theater of the World*, abandons the analogy whenever it ceases to serve its purpose. In the real theater there are rehearsals, and the actors' lives are different from the roles they play on stage. As Wardropper says, "Allegory is a prolonged description of a theme under the disguise of another one which is suggestively similar" (Wardropper, p. 100). The allegorical technique serves the didactic purpose of the *autos* very well. The representation of the body as a castle where the soul lives, with the forces of good and evil struggling for its possession, is an excellent way of giving visual and plastic form to man's spiritual struggle in a way understandable to the least literate, and artistically satisfying to the more sophisticated spectators. Since allegory deals with abstract ideas, the demands of chronology can be dispensed with, much the same as in biblical allegory.

The next play analyzed, *The Testament of Christ (El Testamento de Christo)*, was written in 1582 for the Corpus feast at Toledo.[61] It has certain characteristics of a medieval debate. The three contenders are Grace (representing the New Testament), Scripture (the Old Testament), and Peasant or Ignorant (The natural law), who want to establish which of them is Christ's most worthy heir. Buck thinks that Sánchez de Badajoz's *The Play of the Church (Farsa de la Yglesia)* was its source.[62] In both works one can easily detect a very clear echo of the controversies which took place for several centuries in Spain between the Christians and Jews. In 1582 the author had in mind those Jews who, though officially converted to Christianity, were suspected of doubtful orthodoxy.

In the first part of the play, the three representatives argue their points.[63] Actually the debate is between Grace and Scripture, for the Peasant does not lay claim to anything, although he is also entitled to his sustenance. Scripture wants to keep all of God's possessions to herself. The Peasant asks then, if there is anything left for him because he is really starving (v. 74). Scripture refuses to share anything; Grace, however, says that Christ in His will left food for the needy and the poor. The Peasant is very happy to hear that, for all he really wants is to be satiated (v. 81). When Grace asks if he would be satisfied with bread and wine, he answers that he already has that but is still hungry. With these remarks about bread and wine, the eucharistic element is introduced, becoming the central theme as the play develops.

Since the debate seems to be leading nowhere, they decide to bring in an impartial judge. Faith will preside over the debate, but she calls on Pontif to be the judge. A Master takes up Scripture's case, while a Doctor will defend Grace's. Pontif's decision is in Grace's favor. Christ's New Testament abolishes the Old. Anyone can now share in Christ's inheritance if the person is willing to be born again in baptism. He will receive his sustenance in the form of bread and wine until he is rewarded with the glory of heaven. Scripture and Peasant accept the Pontif's verdict and ready themselves for baptism. The play ends with a song. As can be seen, the *auto* has a very simple line of development. There is no real dramatic action. However, it succeeds very well in presenting the Eucharist as the culmination of God's favors towards men and as the most complete expression of His last will to us. In it Christ leaves His followers the food which will sustain them in this life and be a token of the next one The play reads very well, as the dialogue is very lively. The Peasant provides many humorous comments, which at the end always have a very serious intention.

In summation, the *autos* of this collection are pieces of different artistic quality. They do not represent any advance in dramatic technique over the best plays of the previous collection. Some of them do represent, however, interesting new directions in terms of topics, themes, and materials. Besides the *Códice de Autos Viejos* and the manuscript just studied, there are many other anonymous *autos* of which only brief mention can be made here. Flecniakoska lists about forty-three (pp. 25–34), further evidence of the tremendous dramatic activity around the feast of Corpus. Although it is very difficult to establish the dates of the plays, indications are that they were written during the last two decades of the sixteenth and the first of the seventeenth century. The plays are not without merit, but they do not represent any significant advance in relation to the anonymous collections already analyzed or to the works of the authors to be examined next.

CHAPTER 5

# The Auto and the Professional Playwrights

CONTEMPORARY to the intense dramatic activity of the anonymous collections and related to it in numerous ways are many plays by the authors included in this chapter. Their creations do not always compare favorably with the best anonymous *autos,* but here and there some important changes are introduced whose cumulative effect is the emergence of the sacramental play as a full-fledged and mature dramatic genre.

## I  *Juan Timoneda (1518?–1583)*

Timoneda's love for the theater, indeed for all literature, is beyond question; but scholars are somewhat reluctant to consider him creatively original.[1] Pedroso is inclined to think that none of the Castillian *autos* Timoneda wrote were originally his.[2] Olmedo suspects that Timoneda was somewhat of an opportunist and perhaps even dishonest in using different editions of the same plays to win the good will of the reigning Archbishop of Valencia.[3]

Timoneda published eight *autos.* One of them was in Valencian (*L'Esglesia Militant*); another one in Valencian and Castillian (*El Castell d'Emaús*). These two seem to be unquestionably his. Of the remaining six, one was for Christmas (*Aucto del Nascimiento*) and another for Holy Week (*Aucto de la Quinta Angustia*). My interest here will revolve around the other four. Timoneda introduces these *autos* as "newly composed and added to and improved" by him, or with other similar phrases. The play *The Lost sheep* (*La Oueja Perdida*) is probably the most complicated. Timoneda published it twice, in 1558 and in 1575. In the first edition the author introduces the play as "newly enlarged and improved" by him.[4] The question of authorship is made even more problematic by the existence

93

of an anonymous manuscript of the same play now kept in the
Real Academia de la Historia (Flecniakoska, pp. 34–35). Pedroso[5] and Wardropper, (Wardropper, p. 256) think that the text
of the manuscript was the original play revised by Timoneda.
Juliá Martínez and Flecniakoska, however, believe otherwise.[6]

In the case of *The Play of Faith* (*Aucto de la Fee*) the sus-
picions about Timoneda's authorship are based on two facts:
the subtitle of the play which reads "also called by another
name, *The Pragmatic Sanction on Bread*," and the existence of
a play with this latter title in the *Códice de Autos Viejos*. The
differences among the two are minor. Pedroso thinks that the
*Códice* version is at times better,[7] while Wardropper sees definite improvements in Timoneda's version (Wardropper, pp.
267–71). A similar problem exists with his *Play of the Fountain
of the Seven Sacraments* (*Aucto de la Fuente de los Siete Sacramentos*).[8] Another one, *The Betrothal of Christ* (*Los Desposorios de Cristo*) is introduced as "perfected as much as possible
by Juan Timoneda, the work having been corrupted by bad
writers." All these details seem to establish the fact that
Timoneda felt free to draw upon the large number of anonymous
pieces then existent, to retouch them and to publish them under
his name. Although we do not know enough about the trans-
mission and circulation of the anonymous plays, it seems that
once they were written they were looked upon as common
property which could be changed or improved upon and published by another author as his own.[9]

The most important question for us is the quality of the final
product. Critics are almost unanimous in considering Timoneda's
revisions definite improvements over the originals (Wardropper,
p. 248). He shows a deeper understanding of the poetic exigencies of allegory and greater feeling for the right word and convenient expression. He discards the comic scenes, and the
anticlerical satiric comments take the form of milder admoni-
tions. The plot is more sharply delineated and better controlled,
and doctrine and ideas are more profound and better nuanced
than in the source plays. In cases such as *The Lost Sheep*,
Timoneda's play cannot be called an adaption but a total trans-
formation of the original (Wardropper, p. 256).

*The Lost Sheep*[10] dramatizes the parable of the same title found in Luke, chapter 15, verses 3–7. But St. Luke's story is extremely brief. The last verse of the parable opens the door to its allegorical interpretation, as the Lost Sheep is treated as a sinner. The play puts the parable in a more universal context. The head shepherd is God the Father. His Son, Christ, bought this particular sheep at a dear price, that is, with His crucifixion and death. The sheep had strayed away to the mountains of the seven deadly sins even though she was entrusted to the care of a guardian angel who was helped by the four cardinal virtues and the seven sacraments.[11]

Timoneda tells us in the introduction that this parable can be understood at different levels of meaning: first, it refers to the history of humanity; second, to the history of the Gentiles, and third, to the sinful soul (vv. 41–50). In v. 47, the author seems to indicate that he is not interested in the first two, but in the play itself there are references to the history of humanity, for instance, when he compares the present restless sheep to the first tamer one (vv. 136–40), that is, man before Original Sin; or when mention is made of the mountain of Pride where the first sheep was lost (vv. 359–60, 586–590), that is, the first parents in Paradise. The allusions to the history of the Gentiles are less clear, but the last part of the play from l. 918 on is applicable to this period. Here it is said that the seven sacraments will purify the new members of the seven deadly sins mentioned before.

The third level of meaning, the sinful soul, is naturally the most obvious, and it is clearly maintained throughout the play. This level is the closest to the gospel text: the recovery and subsequent joy of the Lost Sheep. The other levels are not satisfactorily worked out, especially from the poetic point of view. They mar the play by creating a certain amount of confusion in the reader's mind. Significant also are the missed possibilities of dramatizing the moment of temptation and fall, or the wooing back of the sheep by Christ, the Good Shepherd. As Dietz has pointed out, the possibilities for dramatic tension are missed.

A closer reading of the text indicates that the play was written not with the Lost Sheep in mind but rather with the shepherds to whom the sheep were entrusted: bishops and clergy. Tim-

oneda wants to stress two points here: the hierarchial structure
of the Church created by Christ himself as the repository of his
authority (second nucleus of the play, vv. 421–670), and the
serious obligations of the Christian shepherds toward their flocks
of which Christ himself is the ultimate example (vv. 671–977).
Timoneda criticizes the lack of zeal and pastoral responsibility
of the contemporary clergy, especially in the 1558 edition of the
play.[12] This criticism is aimed at the rebellious priests reluctant
to follow the directives and reforms introduced by St Tomás
de Villanueva, Archbishop of Valencia from 1544 to 1555.

The Play of Faith (Aucto de la Fee) is a less ambitious work.[13]
The structure exhibits a very clear line, and the allegory unfolds
with consistency and ease. The complete title reads as follows:
Play of Faith, also called the Pragmatic Sanction on Bread,
Newly Composed in Praise of the Blessed Sacrament, Perfected
by Juan Timoneda. The allegory is based on the second part
of the title: Pragmatic Sanction on Bread, which is the title of
the original play that Timoneda is reworking here.[14] The new
title emphasizes the central role played by faith in the eucharistic mystery. Although the allegory is very well developed,
the psychological processes in man's moral decisions could be
presented more subtly. Man's deception by World has a certain
force, but his conversion is not well motivated. Reynolds says
that "the spiritual meaning of the allegory so dominates the
literal that it can scarcely be read on two levels as is the case
with The Lost Sheep."[15] It must be remembered, however, that
such defects can be corrected in a good staging of the play,
where apparel, stage accessories, and scenery would give the
literal level its proper dimension.

The Play of the Fountain of the Seven Sacraments (El Aucto
de la Fuente de los Siete Sacramentos), a reworking of the older
Sacramental Play of the Fountain of St. John (Farsa del Sacramento de la Fuente de San Juan),[16] is a good example of the
use of the theater for religious and didactic purposes. The
fountain was made by "an artisan who is God and who decided
to become man in the virginal womb" (vv. 203–5). The fountain
has seven spigots which the author describes briefly. The rest
of the play is a catechetical lesson on the excellence of the sacrament of the Eucharist, on the proper way of receiving it, on

the punishment or reward of those who receive it, on the need for faith, and on a series of biblical prefigurations of the Eucharist, ending with a rousing song in honor of the sacrament. The precision of doctrinal concepts throughout the play is very impressive. As the author says in the introduction, it is indeed a serious play. There is really no dramatic structure, and no movement of any kind. It seems to have been written at least in part for an audience familiar with Old Testament figures and events, but very much in need of Christian instruction, perhaps Jewish and Moorish converts.

Among the seven *autos* written about the parable of the Great Supper, Timoneda's *The Betrothal of Christ* is the second one chronologically.[17] The comments after the title, quoted before, made Pedroso suspect the existence of a previous play revised by Timoneda.[18] But no such play has been found. The older one on the same parable is so different from Timoneda's that it cannot have been the source play. In *The Betrothal* I find a certain lack of correspondence between title and content. The play presents a sweeping panorama of the history of salvation, similar to what we find in Calderón's *Life is a Dream* or others of his *autos*. It is a very well balanced composition in which the salient points of salvation history are presented in a beautiful allegory. The wedding banquet, of obvious eucharistic significance, becomes as Dietz has observed, "the focal point of his dramatization." "The lengthy banquet scene becomes a vast allegory of Christ's passion and eucharistic sacrifice."[19] It is a very successful way of expressing the theological doctrine that Christ's passion and the Eucharist are inseparable. The Eucharist is the banquet in which the fruits of Christ's sufferings are given to man. There is a mutual relation of interdependence which in this *auto* is powerfully brought out in a very theatrical and moving way.

It is true that here again Timoneda overlooks "some of the parable's more potentially dramatic scenes," such as the fall and fate of the proud man.[20] Reynolds compares this play favorably with *The Lost Sheep*. I think that it is indeed superior both as dramatic poetry and as theology. There is more abundant and better use of the theater, especially in the central banquet scene. The allegory also has a clearer, less cluttered line than in *The Lost Sheep*. Timoneda has skillfully prepared the scene of the banquet which succeeds very well in making the Eucharist the very center of the history of salvation, past, present, and future. On the basis of the preceding ideas two observations are deemed appropriate: first, Timoneda's plays are definitely superior to the source plays that he is reworking. This opinion is shared by practically all students of Timoneda. Second, his plays do not represent an important or considerable advance when compared to the best anonymous works or even to Sanchez's best. Timoneda is perhaps more civil, learned, and discriminating than others in matters of style. He may have seen sooner than others the convenience of taking out the comic scenes and the profane elements from the *autos*. But these instances of a more refined taste are not enough to put his plays above the best ones we have seen so far. As I have stated, he overlooks scenes rich in dramatic possibilities which subsequent authors would rightfully exploit, concentrating instead on the catechetical aspect of the stories to the detriment of the poetic and dramatic demands. He seems to prefer good religious instruction to good theater.

The dedicatory prefaces, the subtitles, etc., of his plays leave no doubt about his close association with the prelates of Valencia. The *Ternario Spiritual* of 1558 was dedicated to Don Francisco de Navarra, Archbishop of Valencia from 1556 to 1563. The first *Ternario Sacramental* of 1575 was dedicated to St. Juan de Ribera, Valencia's archbishop from 1569 to 1611. These two prelates had been sent there for their extraordinary religious zeal and their intellectual stature. During the first half of the century, the disastrous state of ecclesiastical affairs that developed in Valencia, without a resident bishop for an extended time, forced Charles V to make the momentous recommendation of Tomás de Villanueva for archbishop, which was accepted by the Pope. He was a professor at Alcalá, later made a saint. Philip II recommended Don Francisco de Navarra, previously Bishop of Ciudad-Rodrigo and Badajoz as his successor. He was succeeded by Don Martín Pérez de Ayala, who was soon followed by St. Juan de Ribera, professor at Salamanca and also Bishop of Badajoz.

Conditions in Valencia were extremely delicate both politically and ecclesiastically.[21] These prelates used every means to improve the religious situation: they convened ecclesiastical synods, founded seminaries, took care of the sick, preached, and above all they set their heroic lives as an example to others. Did they also make use of the theater as a means of spreading the doctrine? And, more important, did they have a direct personal influence in the planning, writing, and production of the *autos*? I am definitely inclined toward the affirmative, but I lack the necessary supporting documentation. Circumstantial evidence is abundant. Francisco de Navarra and Juan de Ribera had been bishops in Badajoz coinciding in part and following the creative years of Diego Sánchez de Badajoz. Both bishops were zealous teachers, and the problems in both areas were strikingly similar: a large number of poorly instructed and very restless new converts, and a clergy lacking pastoral zeal.[22] I suspect that the cathedral archives at Badajoz and Valencia have many important secrets to reveal about this period of the *autos*.

## II  *Lope de Vega (1562–1635)*

With Lope de Vega begins a period of well-known playwrights of the secular theater who also cultivate the *auto* with varying degrees of dedication and artistic success. Lope's first sacramental plays are scarcely different from those of the previous tradition. But soon important changes take place which will radically affect the future development of the *auto* and prepare the way for the works of Valdivielso and Calderón. There are about forty *autos* generally considered to be written by Lope,[23] spanning his entire life. *The Soul's Journey* (*El Viaje del Alma*, 1585), one of his earliest pieces called a *representación moral*, a morality play,[24] is written in the traditional five-line, eight-syllable strophe. The eucharistic element is present in the opening section and assumes great proportions toward the end, not so much in the text proper as in the stage directions. But the work remains a morality play where the eucharistic theme has not been well integrated into the total spectacle. It has some uniquely Lopean touches. "The entire lyrical part of the play has a movement, liveliness, and variety of tones which reveal the hand of the great poet."[25]

The auto *The May Pageant* (*La Maya*, 1585) is mostly in five-line, eight-syllable strophes, and the eucharistic element is not very well developed. Similar problems are found in later autos. *The Name of Jesus* (*El Nombre de Jesús*, 1629), a beautiful composition, is rather in the Christmas play tradition. In *Heaven's Heir* (*El Heredero del Cielo*), an excellent play, only the final verses are eucharistic. Indeed, this problem, which repeats itself in many of Lope's autos, is symptomatic of his difficulties in developing an artistic integration of the symbols, metaphors, and poetic possibilities of the eucharistic theme with his more direct lyrical preferences.

Many of Lope's autos reflect a very uneasy situation. They are certainly religious, even allegorical theater. However, I hesitate to call them eucharistic if by that we mean the presence of the Eucharist as the predominant or crowning element in the play, not in quantitative terms but rather the importance which the Eucharist should have in the total context of the play. It is true that in some cases the weaknesses of the written or spoken text are compensated by the representational elements on the stage which compliment the text. An example of this can be found in *The Soul's Journey* and other plays. But even here, from the poetic point of view, one demands a better integration of the theme and an insinuated anticipation of the final apotheosis.

Where critics are unanimous is in praising the lyrical qualities abundant in practically all of Lope's sacramental plays. Sometimes the lyrical tone is maintained throughout the whole play; at other times it is a shorter passage. But all his plays have some memorable lyrical moments of exquisite beauty. Wardropper says that "the characteristics of Lope's comedies—lyricism, love for exotic themes, popular treatment of the material, impulsiveness, episodic nature, unevenness—are also present in all the autos" (Wardropper, p. 276). There are present in his autos a variety of metrical forms never found before.[26] But these qualities are poetic and not necessarily dramatic. In his analysis of the three autos *La Adúltera Perdonada*, *Los Dos Ingenios y Esclavos del Santísimo Sacramento*, and *La Venta de la Zarzuela*,

Wardropper has abundantly illustrated these characteristics with concrete examples (Wardropper, pp. 276–86).

For my part I would like to concentrate here on a different set of works. *Man's Adventures* (*Las Aventuras del Hombre*) is unusual because it shows an aspect of Lope's art with which we are not too familiar: a profound theological dimension associated mostly with Calderón.[27] The play opens with some solemn eight-line, eleven-syllable strophes,[28] as Man is being thrown out of Paradise by the Angel. Man is very conscious of his dignity and honor for he was created just below the angels and in God's image. He is, therefore, entiled to better treatment than that which he is receiving from the Angel.[29] Because of his sin, Man is condemned to death. As he leaves Paradise, Man realizes how nature, symbolized by earth, sea, and thunder, has turned against him. In the midst of these hostile surroundings he asks heaven for some relief. Immediately Consolation appears as a comic character who muses over the future of the world: now it all belongs to one man, but his heirs will fight, argue, and kill for a small portion of it. When Man and Consolation meet, the former is anxious to know whether he will ever find relief, since God is very angry with him. Consolation describes God's plan of salvation. God is certainly angry, but, since He created Man and Man cannot pay for his sin, the Word of the Father will come down to earth, born of a woman, to pay for it. Man says that it was a woman who deceived him and because of her he must eat his bread with the sweat of his brow. Consolation takes up the mention of bread to tell him that he will receive another kind of bread being prepared at this very moment in heaven. So let time pass by very fast so that we can come to that moment when the divine ship (Mary) will arrive loaded with the heavenly bread. This bread will give Man courage and endurance in the passage of this life until he reaches the heavenly palace.

The scene changes revealing several houses with people milling around (the present allegory requires that the world be populated fast); indeed, three thousand years have passed. We are therefore well into the middle of the Old Testament. What is seen is a group of madmen playing, singing, and dancing, while Madness of the World presides, dressed as a queen. Men

are all mad because they do not realize that they are ashes and
dirt. To Consolation's great disappointment, Man decides to
remain there a while. Time, Sin, and Death, dressed as high-
waymen, appear looking for Man. While they wait for him, Time
recounts the history of mankind from Adam on, calling attention
to two symbols of the future Christ: Isaac and the manna. Man
and Consolation now reappear. As Man is very disappointed
with Madness of the World, Time, Sin, and Death take him to
Guilt's house. This is the fate of every one born with Original
Sin. Man is branded as a slave of Guilt as are all of Adam's
children, except that divine Dawn of the Son, Mary.

Consolation promises him salvation in the future. Now, however, he must suffer and eat bread with his sweat until receiving
another kind of bread which will contain God. To while away
this period of waiting, Man tells Consolation the story of his
beginnings: the creation of the world in happiness and harmony
up to his Fall. He implores God to come to his rescue. A cloud
on the stage opens, and the image of Our Lady appears, a sign
of God's concern for Man. Man feels so happy that he falls
asleep. Divine Love (Christ) appears in his dream and takes
Man's grub hoe and carries it on his shoulder. Man exclaims:
"Oh divine farmer, how humbly you carry my faults on your
shoulders and go to the altars of Death . . . like an innocent
lamb. Oh celestial vision, Host. . . ." (p. 63a). Guilt comes to
detain Man, but Christ prevents it, with the result that Guilt
changes his dress into one representing Hope. Guilt has been
conquered by Christ and with His coming the era of Hope is
inaugurated. Time, Sin, and Death realize now what has happened.

The stage changes, and a ship (the Church) is seen carrying
Divine Love, Man, and Consolation while Divine Love explains
some of the future characteristics of the institution whose pilot
will be Peter. To Time's statement that He is soon going to die,
Divine Love answers: "Even though I will leave, I will still be
with her . . . in a sweet token, the same as I am in heaven . . .
and I will designate priests to distribute the divine bread"
(p. 64b). Two angels appear with a chalice. Confronted with
this great miracle, Man asks how to thank God for such favors.
Divine Love answers: "By having faith in me, so that you may

always deserve God's grace here on earth, and God's eternal reward afterward" (p. 65b).

This *auto* is one of Lope's best. The eucharistic theme is very skillfully introduced and developed as an integral part of God's plan of salvation. God's love for man and man's intrinsic dignity are the main reasons for Christ's extraordinary actions. The symbols of man's Fall from grace, the grub hoe and the hard bread, will be transformed by Christ into the instruments of his salvation, that is, the cross and the bread of the Eucharist. The poetic elaborations of these elements, perfectly integrated into the clear outline of the history of salvation presented in the play, are an eloquent proof of how Lope could at times create a very impressive sacramental play.

The seriousness of the theme does not exclude moving lyrical moments; indeed, they are one of the outstanding traits of this *auto*. What I find lacking is the dramatic tension: man's tragic situation between the warring forces of good and evil is almost totally overlooked. Adam's Fall is presented as a *fait accompli*. Later on Man decides to follow Madness of the World, but Lope does not probe into the reasons. We miss here those moments of spiritual crisis which he so vividly described in his more autobiographical poems. Often his *autos* present an unrealistically idyllic view of the religious man and also of the Christian era. In this play he says that the Ship of the Church will be subject to attacks. This accurate prediction is weakened, however, because Guilt, and consequently evil, seem to cease to exist when Guilt changes into Hope. In reality, Guilt and Hope now coexist. Man's tragic situation even today is to decide which of the two to follow.[30] These elements are placed in better perspective in the *auto* to be analyzed next.

In *The Harvest* ( *La Siega,* 1635)[31] Lope dramatizes the Parable of the Weeds, found in Matthew, chapter 13, verses 24–43. At the end of the play Lope calls it a periphrasis (v. 1124), that is, a roundabout way of retelling the parable. In v. 77–80 he says that "here we are dealing in an allegorical way either about His Church, or about the kingdom of heaven, or about the soul." This possibility of different meanings demands constant attention from the reader or the spectator to establish which of the three the author has in mind at each particular moment. In Christ's interpretation of the parable, the sower is the Son of Man, the field is the world, the good seed are the sons of the kingdom, the weeds are the evil men, the enemy is the devil, and the harvest is the end of the world. Though this explanation is the most authoritative one, other interpretations are also legitimate, given the multiple possible meanings of this literary genre. Lope is, then, on safe ground explaining the parable the way he does.

The generous amount of praise which critics have given the play excuses me from dwelling on the skill with which Lope creates the allegory and on the many poetically moving passages throughout the play.[32] Instead I would like to call attention to the excellent treatment of the eucharistic theme. It is an aspect so essential to the poetry and the conceptual content that it is surprising how little attention has been paid to it. As I have observed already, Christ's passion and the Eucharist are intimately related. In the play, Pride calls Christ "a farmer of bread and wine; rich in bread and wine" (vv. 212–13). With the mention of these elements the play definitely assumes a eucharistic direction which the parable does not have in the Gospel. Pride's intention is to sow weeds among the white wheat (vv. 219–20). This white wheat is the Eucharist (and by extension, the faithful who receive it), for the wheat in the fields is not white. Pride will sow all kinds of evil things in this field (vv. 315–24).

Christ knows they are trying to destroy His fields (v. 392), but Wife should not be afraid because His cottage (the Church) is built on a rock (Peter) and defended by another rock (Christ) from which abundant water will come and the bread of life, better than the manna of old (vv. 398–403). Wife asks what will happen to her lambs, since the enemies don't spare even God's lamb (vv. 414–7). Christ answers that some will disperse, but that she should not worry. Before He dies He "will become the wheat and the farmer, in order to feed her" (vv. 431–33). Wife replies in joy: "For such divine favors I cannot thank you enough, you, grace, love, shepherd and food, farmer and bread of love, spouse, blooming rod, mountain, light, chaste lamb" (vv. 434–39). Pride in sowing evil, cannot avoid being sad because in turn "God is sowing the wheat of Bethlehem in a virgin field in order to provide them with bread" (vv. 619–20). Pride and

Envy will sow their weeds and do all they can to ruin God's wheat, and Pride adds: "since it is true that in it are contained death and life, many will eat it who will thereby destroy themselves. And I will act in such a way that, even though God is inviting them to life, few will eat life, and many death" (vv. 873–80). Man's attitude toward the Eucharist is thus presented as the deciding factor of his ultimate destiny. As harvest time approaches it will be a matter of separating the wheat from the weeds (chaff).

The Master farmer knew that there were going to be evils and that they would "sow weeds among the wheat, sweet and divine bite against Adam's bite, hoping to drown the bread, being as it is God in the sacrament" (vv. 972–76). But when Pride and Envy think they have destroyed the wheat (meaning here Christ's death), the Master appears promising Wife all kinds of help during her life here on earth: "And now take a look at my cottage, a good representation of all my treasures, which I leave you as a sovereign testimony of my love. . . . So let him who is thirsty come and I will satiate him with water and holy bread" (vv. 1043–53). Finally it is Pride's turn to extol reluctantly this tremendous sign of love, this fountain of bread, wine and water, through which God found a way to remain with men after leaving the earth (vv. 1059–68). Even though Heresy, Sect, and Idolatry abandon their errors, Pride, of course, will continue to say "endless blasphemies against the bread which has meant death for her" (vv. 1078–79).

The skillful weaving of the eucharistic theme into the texture of the play is indeed impressive. It starts in a very subtle and simple way, gaining momentum as the play advances, until we reach the spectacular apotheosis at the end. The poetic and scenic devices through which this is achieved are placed at the service of the religious doctrine of the play. Together they achieve two very important things: They present the Eucharist as the culmination of the revelation process of God's love to men; and, second, the Eucharist is shown to be the decisive factor in man's ultimate fate. This parable has been turned into an excellent vehicle for the expression of the central role of the Eucharist in the plan of salvation and, consequently in the life of each individual. Theology, drama and poetry are so well integrated here that I must rank this *auto* among Lope's best.

The next composition deserves equally high praise. *Actions Speak Louder Than Words (Obras Son Amores)*[33] was written for the Corpus festivities of 1620. The proverb of the title summarizes the moral of the play, which opens with Human Nature, dressed as a lady, talking with Desire and Hope, her maids. They do their best to entertain her but she is rather disappointed. Although they have been reminding her for centuries of God's promises, these are never fulfilled. She does not lose faith, for she believes in God, and He is one who keeps His word. But she is now subject to the cruel Prince of the World, and her father (Adam) is his prisoner. Desire is equally disheartened. It is true, he recalls, that God promised that one day a certain woman (Mary) would crush the head of the prince, but it is taking too long. Hope, however, recommends patience.

Divine Love now appears with a letter from the King of Heaven in which He reiterates His love for Human Nature. She is overjoyed with this reassurance. Divine Love asks her to reject the empty and futile love of the Prince, advising her to look at some events of the Old Testament for clues about what God will do for her. The first clue is the sacrifice of Isaac, which is reenacted as Divine Love provides the commentary. Lope presents the story for its prefigurative value and for the moral lesson it contains. In terms of the dichotomy of the title, the story is one more word or promise which will find its fulfillment in Christ's passion, when He will climb another mountain (Calvary) carrying another kind of wood (the Cross) to die on. The Angel's promises to Abraham are a reward for his obedience and fortitude, and Divine Love wants Nature to learn this lesson. But she replies that she is in love and cannot cease her lamentations for her absent lover. The theme of God's love, introduced before, presents certain problems to Human Nature's mind. The natural consequence of love is the union of the lovers. But how can God unite Himself to the lowliness of Human Nature? One could well have serious doubts about it if God had not said it, for only God can find a way.

The second nucleus, based on the story of Jacob's dream, will show how this can be possible. Divine Love introduces the scene in a beautiful speech, each strophe ending with the sentence "God can do it, because He is God." God will marry Human Nature, and both will be one flesh. God will put on a rustic dress and become mortal. The clouds will rain the just, heavenly dew will fall on a white fleece (Mary), and also bread of sweet taste will come down. He points to Jacob who reenacts the dream about the ladder which reaches from heaven to earth. During the dream, the King of Heaven makes Jacob important promises. Divine Love comments on them, telling Nature that God can come down and unite Himself with her. Jacob awakes, promising that, if God gives him bread to live and clothes to cover himself, he will recognize Him as God forever. As Jacob exits, Divine Love explains the meaning of the ladder to Nature: God can come down to the world and Human Nature can go up to Heaven. This will become reality when he descends from heaven via the ladder to become man. Human Nature inquires about the bread and clothes that Jacob had requested from God, to which Divine Love replies that God will give Israel manna, bread sweeter than honey, in the desert, and later on, when the world will put on the dress of the Law of Grace, God will give them a bread in which He Himself will be contained. A beautiful lady farmer (Mary) will bake this bread in her womb, and when Passover comes, the Lamb will remain in the bread for those who have faith.

The reenactments of the two Old Testament stories are like windows through which we glimpse God's workings toward man. In this *auto*, Lope emphasizes their prefigurative value, that is, they are promises of a greater reality to come. Human Nature, whose faith in God never wavers, finds them less than satisfying, however, for she is the lover who finds the messages of the beloved an inadequate substitute for His presence. She pleads with Divine Love to tell her husband that she is dying to see Him on earth. She cries now and her tears will be the answer to His letter. When He sees these tears, Divine Love says that He will be unable to delay His coming any longer. In a beautiful religious version of a popular ballad, Nature asks Divine Love to describe her wretched condition and to urge Him to come. Promises are no longer enough. Let the beautiful Virgin be born in whom He will take flesh. Let Bethlehem be called the House of Bread,[34] and let the bread of heaven come to abolish the tyranny of Leviathan. Divine Love hurriedly departs with this message. This first part of the *auto* is a beautiful portrayal of the deep longings of Human Nature in her fallen state, awaiting her redemption. God's promises maintain her faith alive, but only His presence will satisfy her love. Lope gives a very poignant expression of the expectations of the Old Testament by presenting them in the poetic form of the absence of the beloved.

The second part begins with the entrance of Prince of the World. He is angry because his house (the world) is always open to the light of heaven, and hates to see Hope close to Nature. When Hope and Desire remind him of his rebellion against God and his punishment, he argues that he is happy the way he is. Nature retorts that she is not happy with him, because she loves someone else. The Prince responds by putting more chains on her. When Desire reminds him of the promised woman (Mary) who will show God's power, Prince retorts that the times should pass to see if those promises are fulfilled. Then, the Prince enumerates a series of events of the Old Tetament, thus bringing the action to the time of Christ's birth. Hope realizes that the moment has come for the King of Heaven to take away the Prince's power. Although Prince tries to eject her, Nature knows this is impossible. Prince tells Jail and Tyranny to stain Nature and mark her with his brand,[35] but Nature replies that her husband's three nails (on the cross) will take it out; a drop of His blood will cleanse the stain. After Jail and Tyranny lead Nature away, the King of Heaven appears dressed as a pilgrim, accompanied by Divine Love. It is now Christmas, and the Prince cannot understand the great joy on earth. Could this be Israel's new escape from Pharaoh? If so, this time his horses will not drown in the Red Sea. But the King says that His blood will be another Red Sea where those horses will die, and He will take away Nature's chains to put them on the Prince. The Prince leaves the stage in a state of confusion, threatening to meet Christ in the desert.

King and Divine Love approach the jail to see Human Nature, their relative on His mother's side. Nature appears and recognizes Him. Hope and Desire now leave her, for God Himself is with her. The King, however, laments that Hope and Desire must continue living among the Hebrews who do not welcome Him and will kill Him out of envy, even though He is the one in whom all the prophecies are fulfilled. Human Nature, sure of Him, reviews His promises to her: the one made in Paradise when her father (Adam) was told to eat the bread of suffering, the rainbow after the deluge, the sacrifice of Isaac, Jacob's ladder, and the many prophecies. But the best is still to come, for all these were promises and words, and He knows that actions speak louder than words. Human Nature invites the King to her castle to talk about His Passion (of love), to break bread and to have supper together, because, again, these will be actions which will speak louder than words. The King accepts this challenge and promises her even greater proofs of His love. Human Nature, alone on stage, proclaims her faith in God again, and explains that her demands are motivated by her deep desire to be free from the Prince's brand.

Now two doors open on stage, revealing a table with a chalice on it. The King and Divine Love are seated with a pelican between them from whose breast hangs a red ribbon which trails into the chalice. The King tells Nature that, if actions are proofs of love, God giving Himself to her is a proof indeed. Now she can see the best proof He can give her, for He will stay with her in this bread. Nature is overwhelmed. Following this, the two go to free Adam, but the Prince refuses to give him up, because only God can pay the debt he owes. Nature argues that He is coming, He will be the ransom, and Human Nature will be God's spouse, to which he retorts that God must be out of His mind to marry his slave for love.

The King on the cross can be seen on the stage now, as Divine Love orders the Prince to take away Adam's chains, for the second Adam has paid the bail due for the first. The chains fall from Human Nature. Adam appears, putting the chains on the Prince, who is amazed that a dying man (Christ) can enslave him. The King asks Nature whether she is satisfied with His proofs of love. She is, for who else but God would leave heaven to live with her children? Who would give Himself to them in the form of angelic bread? Who but God would die for her? The King invites her to embrace Him, for she is washed now

and clean and will partake of His glory in heaven. He gives her
His grace.

Menéndez Pelayo, in his brief remarks about this play, complained of the small amount of critical attention paid to it.
J. M. Aicardo echoes this opinion. Sanzoles is of the opinion that
the theological dimensions and metaphysical depth make it
one of Lope's best, even though the allegory is somewhat weak
due to its lack of comprehensiveness and vitality.[36] Indeed, this
*auto* gives the impression of an unfinished work. The outline is
most satisfying with the history of salvation presented with great
concision and economy. The proverb of the title gives the play
an original direction. Human Nature uses the proverb to remind
God of what a true lover must do, and to coax Him into action.
Usually it is God who takes the initiative, but Lope sees God's
relationship to man in more human terms. Human Nature is the
lover complaining about the absence of the beloved, unhappy
with mere promises, and demanding extraordinary proofs which
God gallantly obliges. Though the protagonists are different,
the situation is similar to many in Lope's comedies.[37] Poetically
the eucharistic theme is well elaborated and at the end of the
play it assumes its proper dimension as Christ's greatest proof
of His love. The variety of metrical forms contributes greatly
to the overall beauty of the play.

What I miss here is what I find lacking in many of Lope's
*autos*: a fuller rhetorical elaboration of its many beautiful passages, and a more dramatic presentation of man's tragic condition. Defects such as these prompt critics to make statements like
the following by Sanzoles: "In Lope's *autos* there are no conflicting situations (problemática), no thesis; there is no conceptual density; we have only stories (anécdota)." And yet, a
few pages later, he nonetheless affirms that the present play
represents "a gigantic step" in the development of the genre.[38]
An opposite view is taken by J. M. Aicardo, however; in his
opinion Lope's *autos* neither represent a new mode or school,
nor are they a gigantic step in the development of the sacramental plays. In the area of the eucharistic drama, says Aicardo,
Lope never eclipsed the work of his contemporaries as he did
in the secular theater.[39] These conflicting opinions accurately
show the critic's dilemma in assessing Lope's role in the history

of the genre. Few of his *autos* come close to being masterpieces.

It has been said repeatedly that Lope's most successful allegorical works are those based on an already extant allegory, that he is at his best creating the shorter ones, scattered throughout his *autos*, as beautiful parts of an incomplete unit.[40] He seems incapable of creating major allegories, whole plays with the poetic consistency which allegory requires. And yet, Sanzoles himself nonetheless recognizes that *Man's Adventures, Actions Speak Louder Than Words,* and *The Harvest* are excellent works and outstanding contributions to the development of the genre.[41] In my opinion, these plays are more than lyrical elaborations of simple allegories. Lope's *autos* offer a rich doctrinal content dealing with the salient points of the history of salvation and adequately show Lope's capacity to create a beautiful synthesis of man's spiritual history within an allegorical frame and with a eucharistic theme. They also show, as A. M. Cayuela says, Lope's awareness both of the obvious and of the rather hidden connections between the Old and the New Testament. Lope found ways to express them, clearly yet beautifully integrated in the sublime unity of the eucharistic doctrine.[42]

## III   *José de Valdivielso (1560?–1638)*

Wardropper's excellent chapter on Valdivielso still remains the best introduction to his *autos* (Wardropper pp. 293–320). Valdivielso is a meticulous craftsman with an unfailing sense of proportion and balance, an exquisite feeling for language and poetry, and a total familiarity with contemporary artistic currents. He shows perfect mastery of genres as disparate as the religious epic poem, the sacramental play, and the extremely delicate, demanding (and almost exclusively Spanish) poetry *a lo divino.* [43]

During his life, Valdivielso was very well known for his clerical capacity and as an excellent writer.[44] His works later fell into unjust obscurity, probably because of the exclusively religious character of all his writing and, as far as his plays are concerned, because of Calderón's subsequent dominance of the genre. Seventeen of Valdivielso's religious *autos* survive. Of these, some are not really sacramental plays. For example, *The*

*Birth of Our Lord* (*El Nacimiento de Nuestro Señor*) is a Nativity play, and *The Descension of Our Lady* (*La Descensión de Nuestra Señora*) is an occasional piece.

In the foreword to his works, Valdivielso shows the reader, without any rhetorical ambiguities, the confidence he has in the value of his plays: "I do not think that printing these plays will detract from the warm welcome they received when staged, for they won more than the usual applause from the best audiences in Spain" (p. 26). He chose twelve *autos* to be published because of the originality of their content and because some playwrights were passing them off as their own (p. 27). In the dedicatory preface to the Archbishop of Toledo, Valdivielso says that the plays show, among other things: "a christian philosophy, false pleasures unmasked and useful disillusions" (p. 26). In the introduction to the second edition, Guerreiro mentions that one will find these plays "useful and pleasurable, because of their quick-witted style and the piety of their ideas" (pp. 27–28). These passages quoted give us in outline the main characteristics of Valdivielso's plays: a confidence of the playwright in his dramatic formula, a lively and personal style, a doctrinal content of unusual depth, and a Christian philosophy of life, where piety, compassion, and mercy reign supreme.

Valdivielso's greatest artistic merit consists of having achieved a perfect balance in his combination of the dramatic elements. His plays usually have a very clear line of development, where the allegory serves in the most suggestive but unobstrusive way, presenting the moral or theological content. His choice of allegories is unfailingly successful. His contemporaries found that many of them, like the castle, the hospital, and the ship, were easy to understand and follow. The stage directions indicate the care the author took in the proper preparation of scenery and costumes. Never exotic or spectacular, distracting from the doctrine and the message, they help express the ideas of the play more forcefully. The same can be said of this author's frequent use of popular songs, often strategically located to emphasize the importance of some special moment or of the point in question.

The balance and clarity of the action is enlivened by a very personal style, which is deceptively simple. Aguirre has demonstrated Valdivielso's skill in imbuing popular songs and poems with a deep religious content through subtle changes in words and style. Many such compositions appear in his *autos*. The same artistic touch can be seen in the dramatist's constant use of proverbs, puns, and humorous situations presented in a very new and highly artistic way, challenging both to reader and spectator.[45] As for his Christian philosophy, it could well be called a philosophy of love, compassion, and forgiveness. Though his plays are full of references to stories from the Bible, he shows a certain preference for the good shepherd and the prodigal son, or as it is called now, the forgiving father. He mentions these stories often and at very strategic moments. One of his *autos* is called *The Prodigal Son* (*El Hijo Pródigo*).

Perhaps the most impressive characteristic is his convincing dramatic presentation of the psychological processes in man's moral decisions. The resources of the stage are used very well for the portrayal of the insights of the theologian. In essence, Valdivielso's view of human nature is not very different from that of other dramatists: Man enjoyed a state of total happiness lost through the wrong use of his will, and is the victim of his rebellious faculties and senses. He falls into sin and would be hopeless if it were not for God's love and compassion which knows no limits. Love, not justice, always wins out. In Valdivielso's theater, none of the characters is ever damned. This vision is not a naive concept of human goodness, however, but a radical christian optimism based on faith in God's concern for us and his eagerness to save us from the deception of our senses and the insidious, deceiving appearance of worldly things.

These traits are common to all his *autos*. In some, these characteristics are very forcefully brought out, as is the case of *The Prodigal Son* (pp 44–49).[46] Regarding this *auto*, Wardropper has observed that 'Valdivielso omits the emphatic reference to the Eucharist with which his other *autos* end" (Wardropper, p. 297). *The Prodigal Son* mentions, of course, the banquet of the parable, but with little elaboration. It is almost as if Valdivielso did not want to belabor the obvious. Indeed, I find similar subdued treatment of the Eucharist in most of these *autos*. In *The Phoenix of Love* (*El Fénix de Amor*) references to the Eucharist are so few that one is tempted to deny it the title of *auto* and admire it as a beautiful religious version (*a lo divino*) of a cloak and dagger play. But the Eucharist is part of the final union between Christ and Soul, and this sacrament is the token of His love for her.

Wardropper and Dietz have already analyzed the *autos, The Prodigal Son* and *The Pilgrim*; Flecniakoska and I have studied elsewhere *The Madmen's Hospital* and *The Shepherdess from Plasencia*.[47] In the next few pages, therefore, I will present an analysis of three other plays from his remaining *autos* and thus show in more detail Valdivielso's mastery of the genre. Valdivielso's capacity for fine psychological analysis of the soul's faculties and of the human senses in matters of faith is patent in his *auto, The Free Captives* (*Los Cautivos Libres*).[48] After Adam's Fall, the faculties seem disoriented and in disarray.[49] Will loves what is good and consequently loves God because He is the absolute good, but Will would like to understand Him. The personification of Understanding replies that Will can love Him without understanding Him. Memory then tells Will that, if he can only find Faith, he will find everything he wants.

The scene shifts and the characters proceed to Faith's palace (the Church) whose door is guarded by St. John the Baptist, the precursor of Christ, symbolically at the entrance to the New Testament. Sight arrives but, being told she cannot enter unless she blinds herself, she freely accepts becoming a captive. John reveals that Taste, Smelling, Touch, and Hearing are already Faith's prisoners, happily awaiting their rescue (vv. 195–98). Sight will have to wash herself in the fountain at the door (Baptism). Doubt arrives as a knight, but, refused entrance, challenges Faith and all her followers to a fight, including that "worshipped bread which I cannot understand" (vv. 299–300). Doubt then leaves to wait for an answer, and Memory, Will, and Understanding arrive. John guides those who come "looking for the true good" (v. 350), explaining to them the conditions: enter in darkness (*a oscuras*) (v. 369). Will and Memory decide to go in. Understanding follows but somewhat reluctantly, and they wash themselves at the entrance (v. 391). The stage changes and we are inside the palace. Faith appears with Hearing and Sight, her captives, and two songs underline the convenience of having these two senses prisoners in matters of faith. St. John escorts the new captives, Memory, Will, and Understanding to Faith, who tells them their responsibilities: "Your obligation, Will, is to love; yours, Understanding, to believe; yours, Memory, to remind both what they have to do" (vv. 496–99). In this way they will triumph over themselves, and Faith along with them.

In the next scene, Faith appears in triumph in the upper part of the palace, which is described by John. Faith has captured man's faculties throughout the world. Her greatest trophy is a chalice with a host, because the most precious sacrament is a mystery of faith (vv. 644–47). But this triumph is not complete, for Doubt has entered, disguised and clinging to Understanding (v. 669). Doubt wants to decipher this mystery of faith (the Eucharist). The consequence is that Understanding will continue having doubts. Doubt advises him to run away from Faith's jail. Understanding admits God's existence and the reality of the Trinity, Christ's Incarnation, passion, and resurrection, but finds no satisfactory answer for the mystery of the Eucharist (vv. 790–93). Faith arrives, just when Understanding is about to flee, inquiring of Will and Memory how they are faring. Both are very happy. Understanding, however, is very sad, and Faith asks him the reason, since all who eat her bread are happy (vv. 843–44). They discover Doubt's presence, and Faith and Innocence accept her challenge. How can Christ change into bread (vv. 881–84)? How can a body be in two places at the same time (vv. 945–46)? Faith and Innocence answer these and other similar questions with the familiar arguments, adding that it is unwise to ask too many questions; better to eat and be silent. Ultimately it becomes a matter of faith in God's omnipotence, wisdom and truthfulness. Since Understanding accepts all three and it is God who said He was in the Eucharist, Faith urges Understanding to worship the bread "because it is the bread of life, and the bread of understanding" (vv. 1051–52). He finally accepts, "anxious to leave such obscurity" (vv. 1069–70), and Innocence announces that the Rescuer and Redeemer of captives cannot delay much longer. Faith rejoices "because I want all of you to eat happily at my table" (vv. 1076–77). Innocence agrees, since tribulations are easier to bear when one has enough bread to eat. Everyone leaves except Doubt who encourages Sight not to accept the Eucharist. Sight answers: "I see bread but I worship God" (v. 1119). Since the present captivity is going to end very soon, she will then go to enjoy the glories of this mystery (vv. 1136–39).

Hearing now announces the Rescuer-Redeemer's arrival. He left the harbor of heaven in a light galley; the mast is the cross, the sails are the wings of the Holy Spirit, the oarsmen are angels, and the star is Mary. Arriving with His light, He changed the obscurities of Faith into Elysean Fields of clarity, and rewarded Will, Memory, and Understanding. After having eaten the hidden food with Faith, they are to dine with Christ. The Redeemer appears, and Sight finally sees him face to face. As a galley comes into view, they prepare to embark. On it are Christ, St. John, the three faculties, and the five senses. As they depart with music and gun salutes, doubt surrenders to Faith, before such a glorious spectacle, and Faith, thereby, frees her from her errors.

The allegory, taken from the all-too-familiar experience of captivity,[50] is very subtly presented. It provides the outline for the action but never overwhelms the theme which is being considered. The captivity we are dealing with is of a very special kind. As mentioned before, allegory is the substitution of one thing for another which is suggestively similar. The suggestive character can be positive or negative; in most cases it is positive. However, in the present *auto* it is negative. Freedom from Faith is equivalent to confusion and sadness, while submission to her brings man purpose and happiness. This aspect of the play is very well brought out by its tripartite structure. Before the coming of Christ, man's condition was one of confusion and disorientation. After His coming, man's faculties and senses have direction. John the Baptist explains the condition for enjoying the safety of the palace of Faith: they must surrender to her mysteries. John represents the dividing line between the Old and New Testaments. In the Christian era, even the faithful man is not free from doubt. But his captivity is a joyful one because of the presence of the bread, which lessens man's disarray and tends toward his final liberation in heaven. The coming of Christ, associated with Christmas symbols, also represents His second coming in this *auto*. The Eucharit is the prophetic sign

of the second coming and tends towards it as toward its fulfillment.

This *auto* is a good example of Valdivielso's easy command of
the inner workings of our faculties and senses in matters of
faith. To portray their relationship better, the author makes
them the protagonists of the play, Will being the most important
of the faculties, and Hearing, the most important of the senses.
The complicated web of the different forces at work in the act
of faith is presented with great sincerity. Faith is not arrived at
easily. Faculties and senses make forceful demands that must
be satisfied before the peace of faith can be achieved. It can
lead to dramatic moments of temptation and fall, as can be seen
in Valdivielso's other works. Here, though the dramatic element
is not absent, what predominates is the convincing psychology
of the play and the fine portrayal of the interplay between man's
faculties and senses and the demands of faith. The play has a
certain similarity to the way some mystic writers describe the
process of the submission of the senses. The Eucharist is at the
very core of the play: it is the object of faith par excellence,
challenging our faculties and senses; it is also the external reward to those who accept it. This was the lesson Valdivielso
wanted to impart. Faith brings joy and final happiness to those
who submit their faculties and senses. The teaching is positive
Love predominates and there is no emphasis on fear. The author's style is direct and simple, and as in most of his plays,
popular ballads, songs, and proverbs are used with uncanny skill.
Valdivielso, in a most natural way, gives them a new spiritual
sense, a mark of true sensibility and art.

*The Tree of Life* (*El Arbol de la Vida*) refers to the tree in
Paradise mentioned just before the tree of knowledge of good
and evil (Gen. 2:9).[51] From the latter, Eve and Adam ate the
forbidden fruit. The tree of life is a prefiguration of the true
tree of life, the cross of Christ; and its fruit, Christ Himself,
especially in the Eucharist, which in its turn is a prefiguration of
the fruit of the tree of life, with which the faithful will be rewarded in heaven. John the Evangelist uses the expression in
this sense in Revelation chapter 2, verse 7; chapter 22, verses
2, 14. The play opens with Mercy trying to subdue a desperate
Mankind, screaming at the doors of Paradise from which he

has just been expelled. Mankind wants to go back and eat of the tree of life to counteract the ills he is suffering from eating of the other tree, for Mankind realizes what he has lost. In answer to his desperate calls, Justice appears at the door "with a sword of fire" (v. 32+).[52] If it were not for Mercy's protection, Justice would kill Mankind instantly. Death is what crime deserves. Mankind answers that he will not give up the idea of eating the fruit of life which will restore the life he lost (v. 40–44). Mercy, however, says she will take him to a better Paradise and a better tree of life (vv. 61–62), and as Justice leaves, Mankind wonders how he can have his lost happiness restored again. Mercy replies that he can acquire it by being patient and opposing his enemies, Guilt, Ignorance, and Death. Meanwhile, Mercy will look for the proper ground on which to grow the tree of life (v. 104).

Ignorance enters teasing Mankind. By eating he became an ass (v. 133), so now let him work. Mankind could have lived doing nothing but eating and resting, for he was the viceroy of air, fire, earth, and sea, that is, the four elements of the universe. Now he is exiled for eating an apple (vv. 144–49). Guilt appears dressed as the devil and Mankind trembles; Guilt is "the son of the will and of the desire" of Mankind (vv. 166–67) and the father of Ignorance (v. 194), and they are constantly in disagreement. Immediately after Death comes "the one who is not" (v. 212), who calls herself God's clemency (v. 246). Ignorance suggests that she should plead with God to restore Mankind to his former state. Death answers that she will bestow on him an even better state, for a grain of wheat will die but rise and defeat Death (vv. 262–66). Thus Valdivielso subtly introduces the motif of Christ's death, the cause of our redemption. Guilt curses Mankind and gives him unwelcome chores, among others, "you will eat the bread of sorrows kneaded with tears and drink wine watered with drops of your sweat (vv. 292–95). When Mankind still hopes to eat from the tree of life, Guilt and Death decide to take revenge on him, and Mankind describes the miserable state he has created for himself: "prisoner of Death, prisoner and branded by Guilt; bedeviled by a woman and deprived of his sense by Ignorance" (vv. 240–44).

The next section (vv. 352–479) which takes place at the entrance to the Hall of Decisions, i.e., the throne of God, is essentially a medieval debate between Justice and Mercy over man's fate.[53] As each proposes to plead what their names signify, they argue and fight. When Mercy suggests that the Prince (Christ) become man and die, their argument grows so loud that the Prince appears at a high window and promises to come down. Justice angrily retorts that if He becomes man, He will have to die. And Mercy answers happily: "If I see him lifeless, I will also see Him risen, and then I will see man, his sins forgiven, eating from the tree of life" (vv. 476–79). Mercy has won the argument for man.

The following section (vv. 480–734) presents Mankind lamenting the disorder he brought to everything in the universe. Mercy advises him to beg God and the four elements to be good to him. He calls on Earth and she appears; yet, all she can offer is a piece of ground to bury him. He calls on Water and when she refuses to give him anything, he beseeches Air, but she threatens him with snow, hail, stones, and plagues. Last, Fire has only thunder and lightning for him. Beside himself, he begs God to protect him. The answer, "Let God take care of you" (v. 659), is somewhat ambiguous. Mankind, however, understands it as a prophecy of things to come and bursts forth in a long prayer. Among other things he asks for another Paradise with a better tree of life (vv. 697–98): "So let the virgin land, watered by clean rain, bring forth the tree of life, the tree of salvation" (vv. 711–14).

The next nucleus (vv. 735–954) is the continuation of the previous debate between Justice and Mercy, with the Prince already present. He has decided to descend to earth and become man to help Mankind. Although Justice thinks this is too humiliating for the Prince, Mercy perceives it as a sign of true love. He will come so that, if Mankind ate Death in one tree, he will eat life in another one (vv. 875–78). When the time comes, Mercy runs to prepare the inn (Mary) while Justice goes to ready sufferings, cross, and death. The Prince is anxious to start his voyage "to become the tree of life so that he can give it to the sinner" (vv. 951–52).

In the next section (vv. 954–1265) Guilt and Death are surprised to hear Mankind sing as he works for his hope of forgive-

ness. Guilt suspects that God will become man, remembering
what God said after the Fall. Now the weeks of Daniel have
passed, and in Nazareth a baby girl has been conceived without
Original Sin. They have not finished talking when Ignorance
tells them that Christ has been born. Guilt and Death decide to
invite World to give battle to the newborn, but Ignorance warns
that there are three against them (the Trinity), and that just
one of them, tied of hands and feet, will kill them with a bite
(vv. 1032–36). Mankind appears followed soon after by the
Prince "dressed in red" (v. 1057 +).⁵⁴ Mankind asks for forgiveness, the Prince addresses him as the Lost Sheep in a very
moving encounter, during which the Prince tells the servants
to give Mankind a ring and a stole so that he may eat happily.
Once his sins are forgiven, Mankind will eat with Christ (vv.
1083–87). Justice suddenly enters telling the Prince to drink the
chalice and cup of His passion, and Guilt and Death also appear.
Guilt cannot touch Him but will kill Him with the help of Death.
The Prince asks how can they treat Him as a thief, and Guilt
answers that it is because He is the bondsman of the thief who
stole the fruit in Paradise. After the Prince leaves, Mankind
relates to the audience what they are doing to Him off stage.
They rip the bark off the tree of life, and then He dies, soon to
rise again. The tree of life is blooming (v. 1258) like the palm
tree, and between its golden leaves can be seen hanging chalices
and hosts (vv. 1262–65). The stage directions for the final scene
say: "In the upper part of the stage the Prince appears close to
a tree with olive and palm branches, and there are chalices and
hosts hanging from it. He holds in his hand a chalice with a
host. Mercy and Justice hold a sword crossed with an olive
branch. Guilt and Death are chained at their feet" (v. 1277 +).

The Prince addresses a long speech to Mankind, in which the
different motifs of the play are summarized and given final reso-
lution: Come to the Paradise you lost. You will find Mercy, not
Justice at its door, not serpents but saving remedies. Instead of
Eve you will find Ave (Mary), and instead of the forbidden tree
with the poisonous apples, you will find Me, the tree of life. If
once you tried to be God by eating you can succeed now, for
this food deifies. Come; I will be waiting for you in Church
where you will tell me your sins, and, once forgiven, you will

eat heaven and glory (vv. 1278–1313). The play closes with Mankind's invitation to all creation to thank God for His love.

From the point of view of dramatic poetry, this is one of Valdivielso's very best plays. The development of the metaphor of the title has the consistency, tightness, and beauty of a well-wrought poem. The *auto* covers man's history from his Fall and total confusion to his redemption and total illumination. By rebelling against God, man brings upon himself chaos, suffering, and death from which only Christ's love, suffering, and death will deliver him. The play follows a simple line with a well-developed biblical allegory and a clear moving message. The action flows easily, and story, action, and message are well blended. They trace the outline of the history of salvation in such a way that the movements actually correspond to the three moments man experiences when he commits a sin: the Fall from God's grace, repentance and forgiveness, and reconciliation with God. God's readiness to forgive and give Himself in sacrifice is one of the most moving aspects of the play. The message, impressive indeed, is very well presented: Man's salvation is possible because of God's love for His creatures and also of their cooperation with His love. Justice and Mercy are equal attributes in God (vv. 851-52), but the latter usually prevails. Man's fate is demanding and hard, but made bearable by the hope that God's love will triumph and that, as a good lover, He will be ready to forgive and rejoice in forgiving. This is Valdivielso's constant message. God's love overwhelms him. The parables of the lost sheep and the prodigal son, so frequently referred to, decidedly emphasize Valdivielso's concept of God as a Good Shepherd and as a Forgiving Father.

## IV  Antonio Mira de Amescua (1574?–1644)

*Peter Telonario* is the only one of the thirteen surviving *autos* by Mira de Amescua available in a modern edition today.[55] The play presents the Eucharist as the heavenly reward to the generous man. The impetuous personality of the main character is somewhat similar to that of the Apostle Peter for whom he was probably named. The protagonist is a man of extremes: From an avaricious rich man he becomes totally destitute for Christ.

His second name, Telonario, recalls the *telonium* (tax office) where taxes and debts are collected.

This *auto* is, to a great extent, a criticism of the lack of charity on the part of the rich, which explains the many references to the parable of the Rich Man and Poor Lazarus (Luke 16:19–31). Peter's house is completely under Avarice's control. Peter boasts "I never gave alms in my life, and I never plan to" (vv. 191–92), and yet he considers himself a Christian (v. 211). Later on, while sitting at his bountiful table, he absent-mindedly throws some begging pilgrims a piece of bread, an oversight on Peter's part, but the consequences are enormous. During Peter's sleep he sees Charity and Avarice debating about the meaning and value of Peter's action. Justice then appears, and Peter dreams he is before God's tribunal. He cannot remember any good works which may save him. Charity, however, tells Justice about the bread he gave the pilgrims. On the merits of this good action, Peter is not condemned for the moment, but told to be more generous and to take his Christian calling more seriously.

After Peter's conversion the emphasis is put on his Christ-like poverty. He gives away all his possessions, becoming a slave to a shipmaster, who sends him to buy fruit and bread for the voyage. He meets Charity in a garden, a symbol of spiritual sanctity where the fruit "tastes like the bread of heaven" (v. 943). But no mention is made of the bread he was supposed to buy. Peter dies, and in the last scene we see Christ sitting at a table with a chalice and a host. Peter is kneeling behind Christ. The message is summarized in the song: "This is the reward for him who gives alms, even if he had been a great sinner, provided he repented." (vv. 1011–14). The table of the rich at the beginning of the *auto,* the table of the Eucharist at the end, together with the piece of bread Peter gives the pilgrims, all offer possibilities for poetic treatment that would give consistency and beauty to the play. But Mira ignores them. The author's main preoccupation is to praise charity and criticize avarice, without paying too much attention to the consistency of the poetic treatment of the theme.

I fully agree with Wardropper who says:: "In spite of the allegorical form, it is difficult not to conclude that the play was conceived as a comedy" (Wardropper, p. 328). Valbuena, who elsewhere seems somewhat ambivalent, is right when he says that in *Peter Telonario* "the plot is very simple, there is no complete blending of symbol and the thing represented, and the development of the action does not measure up to the greatness of the idea. . . . A powerful unity is never achieved."[56] I encounter similar problems in other plays of Amescua. For instance, in his *The Greatest Human Pride (La Mayor Soberbia Humana), The Heir to Heaven (El Heredero),* and *The Prince of Peace (El Príncipe de la Paz),* among others, the eucharistic theme appears at the very end without previous preparation, and without elaborating its relationship to the content of the play. From the dramatic point of view, mere juxtaposition of different elements is not quite enough. Mira's approach to the *auto* never crystallized into a coherent dramatic formula. The variety and novelty of the topics used in his plays are more impressive. Several, including *The Inquisition (La Inquisición), The Examination of Christ (Las Pruebas de Cristo),* and *The State Treasury and Mount of Piety (El Erario y Monte de Piedad)* are based on the nature and workings of contemporary religious or civil agencies. *The Oath of the Prince (La Jura del Príncipe)* is based on the oath taken by Prince Baltasar Carlos, an event that took place in 1632, the year the play was written. Though references to contemporary institutions and events abound in previous *autos,* they never assume elsewhere the dimensions acquired in Mira's works.

The audience's familiarity with the topics presented makes the doctrine of the play clearer and the impact greater. The institutions and events mentioned appear in a very positive light. The aim of *The Inquisition,* for example, is "the exaltation of the Spanish Inquisition which carries on a bloody and victorious struggle against the heresies which foreigners are trying to introduce in Spain."[57] *The Oath of the Prince* has a similar purpose, for ultimately it deals with "Spain's struggle against the Protestants who are threatening her dominance on land and sea."[58] In *The State Treasury and Mount of Piety,* Mira tries to show that the contemporary economic problems "are a direct consequence of the actions of 'heretics' and other enemies of the faith." [59]

The allegorical disguise does not succeed in giving the dramatized topics a more abstract and universal meaning. Heresy appears in previous works as one of the many possible manifestations of the Devil, sometimes with specific references to the Protestant heresy. But Mira goes much further than that, seeing it as the main enemy of Church and State alike. He wants from his audience not only loyalty to the faith but to the Spanish monarchy and institutions which defend the faith. At times his religious message falls far behind his political zeal.[60] Though these plays are essentially flawed by the predominance of their political elements, references to specific institutions and concrete political events opened up new possibilities which Calderón would successfully explore. In this sense, Amescua can be considered a bridge between Lope and Calderón.[61]

## V   Tirso de Molina (1583–1648)

Tirso de Molina, who so successfully followed and defended Lope's dramatic innovations in the *comedia*, was apparently unable to do the same in his *autos*. After reading the few plays he wrote, one can easily imagine how uncomfortable he must have felt with a genre whose technique he never quite mastered. *The Divine Beekeeper* (*El Colmenero Divino*), probably his first *auto*, describes the relationship between Christ and the Soul under the allegory of the Beekeeper and the Bee.[62] Wardropper considers the allegory both original and beautiful, although even here Tirso's development leaves much to be desired. The play unquestionably is one of Tirso's two best *autos*. Its allegory could well illustrate God's concern with the soul's works of sanctity, but it becomes inadequate when representing the personal relationship between Christ and Soul as that of two lovers. However, our difficulty in accepting the Bee as a plausible representation of the Soul would probably diminish in a good staging of the play, where the role would of course be played by an adult.

Although *Our Lady of the Rosary, the Heavenly Sponsor* (*Nuestra Señora del Rosario, la Madrina del Cielo*)[63] bears the title of *auto*, it is in reality simply "a religious play in one act." (Wardropper, 321). *Much Good May It Do Him!* (*¡No le Arriendo la Ganancia!*), more than an *auto*, is a prolonged satire of contemporary abuses among the high nobility, a common theme in many of Tirso's works. The eucharistic elements are only incidental. Their obvious purpose is the denunciation of the conduct of the men at court, their ambition and their touchy sense of honor. Blanca de los Ríos sees in the play many auto-biographical references which undoubtedly contribute to the character of the play as an occasional piece.[64]

*The Identical Brothers* (*Los Hermanos Parecidos*), presented at Toledo in 1615, and generally considered Tirso's second best[65] *auto,* presents the history of salvation from the moment of man's creation to his redemption by Christ. Boldness, Son of the Devil (vv. 15–20), hopes to gain entry into the house of Man, who has been named by God ViceRoy and Governor of this world, and is making his solemn entrance that day. The four continents accept his rule.[66] Immediately Vanity (Eve) comes to visit him and insists that he eat the forbidden fruit, arguing that man was created in God's and the Trinity's image. By eating the fruit, his dignity would become infinite (vv. 281–82). These are the two elements which give the *auto* its tenuous unity. The middle section is more ingenious than poetic. Boldness, Desire, Deceit, Vanity, Covetousness, and Envy entertain and help Man spend his time in different illicit games. As in any game, someone has to pay. The theme of paying, important at the end, is thus introduced here. God's Justice is announced as coming to take Man to task. He leaves without sharing his earnings with Envy and the others, who go searching for him.

Fleeing from Justice, Man encounters Christ dressed exactly like him. The theme of likeness between Christ and Man is elaborated here. Christ became like us to save us and to give Himself to us as food. He tells Man: "Come, my identical brother, and if you ate of the forbidden fruit in order to be like God, this is the tree of life: if you eat from it you will be like God" (vv. 902–6). The final song is a summary of the play's meaning: "God-made-man pays because of His likeness to man. Happy a thousand times such likeness!" (vv. 940–42). The theme of likeness is well presented poetically, but not adequately developed. The middle section, portraying man guided by his sinful pastimes before Christ's redemption, is rather ineffective. The satiric comments here, neither as extensive nor incisive as in the previous *auto*, do not contribute to the quality of the play either. Furthermore, there is a certain coldness, a lack of religious fervor, as it were, that betrays Tirso's uneasiness in this dramatic genre.

*The Nymph of Heaven* (*La Ninfa del Cielo*), staged in Seville in 1619, an allegorical version of Tirso's three-act play of the same title,[67] is a morality play rather than an *auto* which tells the story of Soul, who, after falling in love with Sin, repents and returns to Christ. He welcomes her as His spouse, giving her, among other things, His own Body (the Eucharist). The play is significant for literary history because several of Calderón's *autos* were allegorical versions of his own three-act plays. Tirso's *The Nymph of Heaven* can thus be considered an important precedent.

In *The Cretan Labyrinth* (*El Laberinto de Creta*), Tirso dramatizes the classical legend without being able to mold it into a convincing allegory.[68] Wardropper observes that "the scrupulous adherence to a legend, whose inadequacy as a vehicle for the eucharistic dogma is evident, deprives the work of its value as a sacramental play" (Wardropper, p. 322). The defects of the play should not be blamed on the legend, however, but on Tirso's treatment of the material. Calderón would show in *The Labyrinth of the World* (*El Laberinto del Mundo*) what could be done with the same elements. As with many allegories, the duty of the dramatist is to choose those elements which best serve to illustrate and poetically enrich the theme of the play. By not exercising this discriminatory function, Tirso ends with a maimed legend and a poor allegory.

To apologize, perhaps, for his inability to realize the obvious artistic possibilities of the material, Tirso has Theseus explain the legend and its allegorical meaning at the end of the play. Following the work, Tirso added a few paragraphs of information on Crete, Minos, Minotaur, Daedalus, and Theseus. He begins by saying: "I am including here what I have found in several authors about the characters taking part in the *auto*, for a better understanding of the play and for the satisfaction of those who, not having read the original fable (*lo material*), may want to understand its metaphoric meaning by knowing it."[69] At the end we find this eloquent phrase: "In the present *auto* I have made use of most of this legend, moralizing almost everything, as one can see in the play."[70] The small number of *autos* he wrote, and the shortcomings of those same plays as eucharistic drama, seem to indicate either a lack of understanding of the genre or a lack of interest in it. Tirso never approached the brilliance and success he achieved in his three-act plays, whether secular or religious.[71]

CHAPTER 6

# Calderón (1600-1681) and After

CALDERÓN de la Barca is the undisputed master of the genre, both in terms of the number of *autos* he wrote and the high quality of so many of them. Equally famous for his three-act dramas, Calderón is a man of the theater, working within the previous tradition but with such strong personal traits that his plays read like original productions. Born in Madrid in 1600, his first play was produced in 1623; 1634 is the year of his first dated *auto*. He cultivated both genres until 1651, when he was ordained a priest. From 1648 until his death, he was commissioned annually by the Corpus Christi Junta to write two *autos* for the festivities. As Wilson states: 'The resulting body of some seventy works is an achievement almost as monumental as that of his dramas.'[1] Calderón took great care in the revision and accurate printing of his *autos*, so that the text of his works is in far better condition than that of most of his predecessors.

Several attempts have been made to classify Calderón's *autos*,[2] generally not very successfully or usefully. However, they indicate clearly the wide range of sources and motifs present. It is true that in the *autos* of his predecessors topics of the most diverse sources can also be found: biblical, historical, mythological, folkloric, and literary. Calderón knew these works well and availed himself liberally of the materials at his disposal. To begin with, he elaborated them more fully and established closer relations between these materials and the Eucharist. Comparing Calderón's *autos* with those of the previous tradition, his sacramental plays appear to be an original realization of the possibilities implicit in this form. Calderón reworked previous materials, developing a personal dramatic formula whose characteristic notes are a very learned literary style, a great clarity of structure, and a successful way of creating an intense theatrical effect with the help of music and stage directions. And so, while some of his predecessors' *autos* are weak and tentative, Calderón, with the same materials, created perfect masterpieces. The sources of his philosophical and theological ideas are indeed wide-ranging. Parker observes that Calderón "is . . . an eclectic, taking from here and there what best suits his purpose. The general framework of his ideas is Augustinian."[3] A few lines earlier he calls Calderón "the dramatist of Scholasticism in general." It is possible that Calderón did read the works of the Scholastic writers. I tend to believe, however, that his major sources were the writers of that rich and famous period of Spanish theology, that is the sixteenth and seventeenth centuries.[4]

Calderón belongs to no particular school; he is eclectic and middle-of-the-road, so to speak. The author's best guide is *sentire cum Ecclesia*, that is, he follows the common doctrinal tradition of the Church. Thus, his *autos* are a means of teaching moral and religious doctrine, and of moving wills to a deeper worship of God in and through the Eucharist. He teaches not dogmatic theology but moral and religious doctrine, aimed at creating a deeper devotion. His plays show a marked preference for the learned style ( *culto* ) and for the best characteristics of contemporary metaphysical poetry. As Wilson states: "Calderón's dominant mode is rhetoric."[5] We find in his *autos* the added difficulty of a constant use of technical terminology taken from philosophy, theology, and exegesis.

The tight unity which critics have admired in Calderón's longer plays is also present in most of his *autos*. One of his contemporaries talks of "the admirable way in which he arranges things, thereby bringing his plays up to the level of a science which proceeds as a perfect syllogism: it makes a statement, it then presents the objections and ends with their solution. . . . This Calderón did at an even higher level in his *autos*."[6]

This quality of order is a result of the great care the author took in setting down the principles from which the rest of the action flows with the inevitability of a perfect syllogism. J. M. Cossío, studying what he calls rationalism in Calderón, affirms that the playwright puts the highest value on the human intellect. This is in obvious contrast to the value which ascetic writers assign to the will.[7] E. W. Hesse adds that Cossio's conclusions are applicable to all the genres Calderón cultivated, but Hesse calls this aspect dialectics and casuistry.[8] A. L. Cilveti's book-length study of the "rationality" of Calderón's drama, *Life Is A Dream* is the best and most exhaustive study of this aspect of his art. His conclusion is most important for the understanding of Calderón's *autos*. Says Cilveti: "The logical structure is the one which gives us the key to appreciate Calderón's method and thought in the play *Life Is a Dream*." However, "the tragedy of *Life Is a Dream* consists precisely in the characters' impotence to discover the ultimate reality without supernatural help." They end "by submitting to the influence of faith."[9]

The logic of pure reason is never enough for Calderón, for it is unable to lift man above himself. Only faith can do that, and faith is the acceptance of the supernatural. Calderón drama-tizes vividly here, as he often does elsewhere, the struggle of man's intellect before submitting to faith. His keen interest in man's mental processes appears also in the frequent remarks made in the religious plays themselves regarding the stages the playwright goes through in the creation of his allegories. The *auto, The Greatest Day of All Days (El Mayor Día de los Días)* dramatizes the creative process itself.[10]

For Calderón, the play is never simply the written text. It acquires its full meaning and dimensions only when it is acted on the stage, for, as he says, the written text "cannot convey either the sonority of the music, or the spectacle created by stage devices, unless the reader can conjure them up in his imagination."[11] Though music had been part of the *autos* from their very beginning, Calderón made more and better use of it than any other playwright, defending this practice again and again in the face of intransigent critics, and writing true musical plays. Actually, for Calderón the *auto* was an artistic and moral unit consisting of three elements: theme, poetry, and music.[12] Music is subordinated to the theme. Opposed to popular, sensual music called poison to the ears, spiritual music is a reflection of heavenly harmony and also the voice of divine inspiration.[13]

Calderón's great concern for the appropriate staging of his *autos* is well documented in the special notes (*memorias de las apariencias*) he wrote detailing all the stage devices needed. The production of the *autos* was quite spectacular by this time.

In the beginning of the seventeenth century two carts were used for each of the four *autos* represented. In 1648 an important change took place. From then on, instead of four *autos,* only two would be performed, and the number of carts for each play would be increased to four. The obvious consequence was the major importance thus given to the staging proper. It should be remembered also that from 1648 until Calderón's death in 1681 all the *autos* staged in Madrid were written by him, and all of them needed four carts. Shergold has analyzed the meaning of this decision for the history of the Spanish stage.[14] M. Ruiz Lagos, for his part, has called attention to the importance which the allegorical scenes and other stage decorations have for the understanding of the action.[15]

Calderón, whose interest in painting was deep and discriminating, tried to make the best possible use of an old established custom. Many of these painted allegories, much more than mere decorations, are graphic and very effective summaries of an argument or a chain of ideas. They are essentially cathartic elements used very successfully, especially in the final scenes, to express the preeminence of the Eucharist. E. J. Gates is correct in concluding: "It is evident . . . that Calderón's interest in art was an abiding one. It became an integral part of his drama, and it reflects not only his personal feelings but also the taste of his time—both in religious art and in portrait painting."[16] In Calderón's plays we can probably see better than anywhere else "the theatrical mode which takes over the arts and, generally speaking, all manifestations of life during the baroque period."[17] Calderón also paid great attention to the movements of characters on stage. Quite frequently the stage directions specifically point out the way characters should change places, with precise indications of when and where to stop. Very often they have the fluidity of a ballet. The characters' movements, like the music or the painted scenes, are always intended better to express the ideas enacted. The preceding observations should suffice to indicate Calderón's eminent position in the history of the *auto*. The more one studies his works, the more one is impressed by his total control of all the elements which contribute to great drama. In the next few pages I will analyze two of Calderón's *autos* as a way of illustrating his art.

*The Divine Orpheus* (*El Divino Orfeo*) is one of the so-called mythological *autos*.[18] From the poetic point of view, it is one of his most beautiful plays,[19] which is the reason why I chose to examine it. There are two versions of this *auto*. Calderón wrote the first one early in his career. The source was Lope's comedy, *Orfeo*. Calderón's second and superior version is dated 1663. The play is preceded by a set of instructions (*memoria de las apariencias*) detailing the things necessary for the staging, and a *Loa* or prologue in which twelve characters take part. Eleven carry a letter of the alphabet each which begins a word extolling one of the aspects of the Blessed Sacrament. When all the letters reach the proper order they spell *Eucharistía*. The Characters change places in ballet-like movements and when they stop the same letters spell *Cithara Iesu*. The idea Calderón wants to express is that both human and sacred letters vie with each other in honoring the sacrament.[20] The *Loa* is no doubt intended to be a subtle preparation of the audience for the use of the myth of Orpheus as an allegory of Christ's redemption. That is, human letters, by helping to give poetic form and beauty to the teachings of faith, can also be made to serve a religious purpose. The *Loa* also makes evident the important role that music and ballet-like dancing will have in the play proper.

The *auto* opens with the Prince of Darkness (the Devil) sailing in total darkness through the river Lethe. Man has not yet been created, but the Prince knows this will soon come to pass. Thus, the Devil, like a pirate, will try to take him away. Envy appears. Both will wait for the moment of man's creation; but as of now, "nothing stirs, nothing lives, nothing breathes" (vv. 409–410). A voice heard from the second cart proves to be that of Orpheus (God), and the work of Creation begins. Each of the six days will be represented by a different character. Great emphasis is put in underlining the qualities of Orpheus's voice—harmonious, sweet, with power to draw everything to itself (v. 417).[21] God creates Human Nature, giving her absolute power over all creatures (vv. 535–39). Created in God's image, He will inspire her with His voice.

The Prince and Envy having observed the whole scene, the evil one recognizes Human Nature very well, because he had seen her picture before she was created, that is, in God's mind.

Indeed, she was to be the Prince's queen and also God's spouse, but the Prince rebelled against God rather than accept such a plan. Now the Prince's envy helps to steal this beautiful creature from God (v. 613). To do this, Envy will change into an asp. The Prince also calls on Lethe, who, with his magic voice will accomplish "prodigious" feats (v. 648). Lethe appears dressed as a sailor and will watch the river until he captures Human Nature.

In the next nucleus the Days and Pleasure are dancing and singing before Human Nature and in her honor. In a perfect expression of harmony, rhythm, and joy in all creation presided over by man, all follow God's voice. Human Nature, however, asks them to stop praising her and to sing a hymn to God, instead. Orpheus, returning on stage in answer to their psalm, is now simultaneously God and Christ, who being in love with Human Nature, comes dressed in his best finery (vv. 816–19); he addresses her like a lover, taking her to Paradise where she can live forever, provided she avoids the asp hiding in the grass. She promises always to listen to His voice, and Orpheus and Human Nature exit "holding hands" and surrounded by the Days (v. 893+).

The following scene which has a touch of humor, opens with the Prince and Envy seeking a way to enter Paradise. They decide to enlist Pleasure's help. Seizing him, pretending to be shepherds looking for work, they inquire whose land this is. Pleasure, apparently in fun, tells them "the fable" of the Isle of Thrace and its famous musician, Orpheus (vv. 974–1053). Pleasure, through subtle changes, accommodates the story to the present allegory. According to Pleasure, Orpheus is the musician with the golden voice. Thrace becomes Grace (in Spanish: *Tracia–Gracia*) (vv. 996–98), and Eurydice becomes Human Nature or Human Soul. The Isle where Orpheus lives is so beautiful that it can truly be called a paradise.

Pleasure has not yet finished when Human Nature appears. He directs her to them and leaves. The Prince, who apparently knows a great deal about the hidden meanings of fables and myths, has understood the sense of Pleasure's fable exactly. How could Pleasure think that he could deceive them with the truth (vv. 1055–56)? The Prince knows that Pleasure's fable and all myths have in them a certain kind of truth, veiled perhaps but valid. He tells Envy: "There will be many times when prophets and poets will be in agreement, when they will brush on truths, though enveloped in shadows" (vv. 1068–71). Indeed, there will be an infinite number of cases when sacred writings and human letters will be in agreement as far as their ultimate meaning is concerned, even though they be opposed in their religious function (vv. 1079–82).

To accommodate the fable to the present allegory even more, the Prince becomes Aristeo, who will destroy Human Nature's beauty, while Envy will be the asp. Now the play can proceed. Human Nature enters surrounded by the Days, totally happy, but the singers warn her about the asp in the grass (v. 1135). She meets the Prince and Envy. The latter is an expert on the properties of plants and flowers, and will prove it with an experiment: If Orpheus told her not to eat of that tree, it is because she would be like God. Human Nature accepts the suggestion and eats. The apple is poisoned, and Human Nature goes into a frenzy of pain. The Days, who were always together before, now pass one by one before her, pushed by Envy (Night) in a beautifully orchestrated series of movements representing the passing of time and also of the disorder of all the things created, which now turn against Human Nature. Sin appears as the destruction of harmony. By following Orpheus's voice, Human Nature maintained herself and the whole of creation in harmony with God; by following the Prince's voice, disharmony, chaos, hostility, and death are introduced. Here we are witnessing the death of her soul, not of her body (vv. 1350–52).

Orpheus, who now appears and realizes what has happened, complains of how ill Human Nature has repaid His love. But He is such a lover that he will prove what kind of love he feels by what he is willing to forgive (vv. 1399–1400). He promises to fashion a musical instrument with which he will show that His love is far greater than her guilt, looking first at the tree poisoned by the asp, and then at the other tree in Paradise where life will be found. The instrument, to consist of three parts and three pegs, will be known as Jesus' cither.

When next we see Orpheus, He is carrying a harp in the shape of a cross on His shoulder (v. 1451+), searching for Human Nature whom he will try to attract with His song (v. 1479). He is willing to cross the river Lethe (to die) in order to reach her. When Lethe strikes Orpheus, it is the former who falls mortally wounded, crying: "Woe to me, for I die at the same time that I kill. All my fury falls prostrated at your feet, where death lies dead" (vv. 1557–61). Orpheus (Christ), also mortally wounded exclaims: "My father, my father, why have you forsaken me?" (vv. 1566–67). Earthquakes and confusion follow, and the Sixth Day falls faint, surrounded by the others. The Sixth Day, of course, is Friday, and Calderón points out that it was on such a day when Human Nature was created. It is now restored with Christ's death, also on a Friday (vv. 1589–93).

The Sixth Day slowly recovers, thus indicating Human Nature's recovery. Orpheus victoriously returns in the ship of the Prince of Darkness, standing near the main mast in the form of a cross with death at His feet (vv. 1605–9). When he demands the return of His spouse who is imprisoned by the Prince, the gate of the jail opens, and he is seen singing. Human Nature appears, and the Prince invites her to the ship of life, located in the fourth cart. The ship is generously decorated with white and red pennants depicting the Sacrament, while the lantern of the ship is a big chalice with a host (v. 1669+).

The Prince of Darkness throws a final challenge. It does not matter now if Human Nature has been rescued because, whenever she sins in the future, she will return to him. Orpheus answers that before He leaves He will provide the ship of life with sacraments which remedy any future perils (sins). When Envy wants to know what these remedies are, the answer is the final scene of the *auto*, a true apotheosis of the Eucharist. The ship of the Church appears, bearing the six Days and Human Nature. The Fifth Day, by the main mast, tells Envy that there are seven sacraments but that the most important one is the one instituted on the Fifth Day, that is, on Holy Thursday during the Last Supper (the Eucharist). All the participants join in exclamations of joy and adoration toward the Eucharist. The *auto* concludes with a song where the prophetic and eschatological aspects of this sacrament are expressed: "Let Human Nature board the ship of the Church. Good trip, happy crossing!

Because the ship of the Church is the ship of life. Good trip, happy crossing!" (vv. 1724–29).

*The Divine Orpheus* provides a good example of Calderón's ability to use a classical myth to illustrate the meaning of the Eucharist. From the classical story, Calderón takes its poetic beauty as well as certain details which can be interpreted as paralleling the main events of salvation's history. The story of Orpheus always remains at the service of the story of Christ. Music constitutes an essential element of the play, constantly used to communicate God's message to man and creation, and also to express man's gratitude to God. The movements of the characters are carefully orchestrated to make the meaning of the text more evident. A very striking feature of the play is its tight structure. Contrasting elements are strategically located. For instance, the play opens with the Prince of Darkness in his ship, ready to ensnare Human Nature in the murky waters of the River Lethe. The play closes with the appearance of the ship of the Church where Human Nature finds the sacraments of life. Similarly, the tree of Paradise has its counterpart in the tree of the Cross. Human Nature is created on the sixth day, and she is also redeemed on the sixth day.

This *auto* is one of the most lyrical that Calderón ever wrote, due probably to his use of the classical myth. In *The Divine Orpheus* one misses perhaps the dramatic conflicts so vividly portrayed in some of his other *autos*. On the other hand, the lyrical tone of the work gives the figure of Christ an appeal not often found in Calderón's works. The severity with which He often appears is replaced here by His love and mercy. Calderón's second version of *The Divine Orpheus*, just analyzed, was written for 1663. Fifteen years later he wrote *The Greatest Day of All Days* (*El Mayor Día de los Días*),[22] a far more complicated *auto*, rich in texture and motifs, an outstanding example of Calderón's best art. I will study it in the following pages.

The play could well be subtitled *How to Write an Auto*, for in it we can observe Talent in the process of fashioning a dramatic allegory for Corpus.[23] Talent has come across two readings: one from the gospel of St. John which says that, "unless the grain of wheat falls to the earth and dies, it remains just a grain of wheat" (vv. 12, 24). The other text is from a famous writer (v. 295) whose words, put to music, proclaim that today is the Day of the Lord par excellence, for it embraces eternal ages (*edades eternas*, v. 13). On this day the earth is tilled and watered by dew; the grain is sowed, the ear of grain matures, it is mowed, thrashed, and winnowed. It is also stored in the granary and in the monstrance. Indeed, from it comes the bread which feeds everyone.

The play opens with Talent in a very pensive and confused mood. He hears the sung text when he is reading the verse from the gospel, and wonders about the relationship between both texts. Talent wants to satisfy his curiosity, and as a result a definite train of thought is set in motion. Thought, dressed as a fool, appears from nowhere, telling Talent to cease trying to reconcile both texts because he knows a wise man who can do it for him. This man, a Paterfamilias, is master of everything under the sun. He has a warden here on earth whose authority extends over the four elements (vv. 105–26). His name is Time, and today, for the present allegory, we might call him both Paterfamilias and Time (vv. 161–62).

Calderón, aware that such identification may seem arbitrary to the spectators, voices their misgivings by having Talent ask Thought whether by accepting a fool's suggestion he is not attempting something very foosish. Calderón thereby invites us to observe his creative processes, probably saying that any allegory entails a certain amount of stylistic violence in the development of the two levels of signification. When done skillfully the final result is a work of art; if not, a foolish monstrosity.

In this particular case Talent takes up the challenge and asks Thought to lead him to the wise man, Time. Thought takes Talent(that is, Calderón and the audience) to the very dawn of time, that precise moment when Time wakes the journeymen of life (*jornaleros*, v. 187) because dawn is approaching. Time appears dressed as a head shepherd (*mayoral*), and Talent greets him warmly. Time is pleased to see him and ready to hear his doubts. The stage is then set for a discussion on the relationship between the texts mentioned before. Talent's problem is that he cannot reconcile what the "choir of faith" and the gospel text say, namely, how can it be that in the space of one day the grain of wheat may be able to go from seed, to fruit,

to food (vv. 311–24)? Besides, why is it that this is said only
about wheat? (vv. 273–77). Time answers that, though the
problem may seem serious and difficult, there are several sacred
texts which will provide the answer (vv. 330–33). First of all,
that grain of wheat is not to be understood literally; Talent
should first become familiar with the methods of interpreting
Sacred Scripture. Time instructs him that, beyond the literal
sense, there is the allegorical and, at an even higher level, the
mystical. The seed of the text is not the real and material seed
of grain, but a divine seed; indeed, God's own Word. Proof of
it is the parable of the sower and the seed. Now if we know that
the seed is the Word of God, and that this Word became flesh
and later Bread and Wine (the Eucharist), it would also be
reasonable to accept the existence of such a long day.

Talent accepts all this because Faith so teaches him (v. 383),
but he still cannot see that one day could encompass this long
period; neither can he accept the fact that the grain has to die
in order to be born. Time promises to make all this clear by
explaining the parallel that exists between Christ and the grain
of wheat (vv. 394–95). Before discussing the allegory proper,
it is useful to remember that Time has here three different levels
of meaning: he is the Paterfamilias (synonymous with Providence); he is Time (the sequence of God's unfolding of His
plan to us); and he is also the head shepherd. Calderón has
now given the action the direction he wants; the premises he
has set are acceptable. What is not yet clear is how the play
will proceed toward a successful development of the allegory.
By leaving these questions unanswered, Calderón involves the
audience deeply in the action that follows. Thus, the spectators
will appreciate Calderón's virtuosity much more, and they also
will remember the lesson he wants them to learn.

A regular day, Time says, has morning, noon, and night. Suddenly Natural Law, Adam, and Idolatry call from inside. It is
the beginning of the day, that is, the beginning of the history of
mankind, and the first group of the journeymen of life wishes
to begin work in Time's fields (vv. 422–24). Calderón here
resorts to the familiar parable of the workers of the vineyard in
order to develop the allegory and to make its meaning more
explicit. Time calls Natural Law on stage, and Talent cannot

understand how ancient Natural Law can return. Talent still has a very literal and realistic way of going about things. Time's answer has two parts: Natural Law never really ceased to exist because it was embodied in the two commandments of love of God and of neighbor given by Christ. Second, we are not bound here to a strict chronological order. Thought has the power to bring back to memory the things of the past. In this way Calderón underlines the unity of the different phases of God's plan, and also the freedom from realistic constraints in which allegory naturally operates.

Talent is satisfied, but grows restless, anxiously waiting for the coming explanations. From this point on, the allegory develops rather smoothly, while Talent assumes the role of a critical spectator, voicing the difficulties he encounters as the allegory unfolds. Natural Law, Adam as the foreman, Idolatry, and a group of mowers enter (v. 450+). Adam narrates the beginning of mankind's history, expressing his hope for a remedy. He will, however, accept the salary agreed upon and work the fields with tears and sweat. Time tells him the salary will be five talents (v. 536) plus the assurance of a future remedy. Idolatry simply does not believe it. Time sends them to the best field in the world, a mountain in Judea, virgin land which nobody has touched where their duty is to till this land and to sow in it the grain of God's word (vv. 544–86). Adam does not want to miss the field, and Time gives him more directions, adding that the ranch house (*alquería*, v. 605) is in Nazareth. Because of its good bread, it will be called Bethlehem (in Hebrew, Bethlehem means the house of bread). All go happily except Idolatry.

Talent now voices some problems. If Natural Law is daybreak, what can noon be? Before Time answers, Written Law, Moses and Judaism with another group of laborers arrive, embodying the answer to Talent (vv. 653–74). They come full of hope to work in his field until the Day of Days arrives. When Judaism wants to make sure they will receive a fair salary, Time assures him of that and sends them to the Mountains of Sion. Those of the Natural Law have already prepared the soil there so that the Virgin Land can "conceive and give birth" before the end of the Written Law (vv. 740–43). Thus, they go, leaving Talent still puzzled. How can the Written Law be the continuation of the Natural Law? The answer is simple, according to Time: They are really one and the same (v. 770). The difference between the number of precepts resembles that which exists between the trunk and branches of a tree (vv. 774–80). Talent accepts this but asks who or what is going to be the afternoon and night of this day. A voice (Grace) sings from within, but Time does not recognize it.

Talent and Time, seeing another group of laborers, invite them to enter. Grace and Apostasy accompany the laborers. Time does not know Grace. When questioned about who she is, Grace states she does not know who she is now, but knows who she will be. When Time asks her why she is not working, Grace informs him that nobody hires laborers so late in the afternoon. Time, however, sends them to his fields, with the salary to be settled later. Grace retorts that she will work free (*de gracia*, vv. 859–60). Once the wheat is grown and cleaned, Grace is to bring it to Bethlehem so that these grains (Christ) can give themselves to us as bread. And so they depart. Talent, who cannot understand how Time can trust someone he does not know, is most anxious to learn how all these mysteries will end.

The scene now shifts to the fields where Night (Guilt or the Devil) wonders what Time is planning by sending those groups of laborers. If he is preparing the Day of Days, then she will be the Night of Nights. Night meets the Natural Law group first, along with their foreman, Adam, who petitions God to send His dew, begging the clouds to send the Just One from the sky. Night asks why Adam is not tilling the ground, and Adam, in a series of plays on words, responds that he will not use his hoe because it is made of a piece of iron (*hierro* or *yerro* means iron and error) and part of a tree, precisely the two things which caused him and humankind their present trouble. Therefore, he will not touch the New Virgin Land with it (v. 1011).

As Adam leaves, Written Law approaches, asking Night where she can find the sacred field she seeks. Night answers that there is no such place in the world, but Moses recognizes the field in the distance. They will go and sow the seed which will be blessed from the moment of conception (the Immaculate Conception (v. 1099). They exit singing, just as Grace and Apostasy arrive with their group. Grace asks Night where Written Law is working. Night does not know who Grace is, but Grace recognizes the other immediately, and soon Night realizes who Grace is. As Grace leaves, Night begins planning the destruction, during the Night of Nights, of the harvest grown during the Day of Days.

Suddenly Idolatry enters, asking Night for help, followed immediately by Judaism and Apostasy. Idolatry cannot accept the belief in monotheism; Judaism cannot accept the belief in three Gods (the Trinity); Apostasy cannot believe in transubstantiation (the Eucharist). All decide to leave their respective groups. Night realizes that hate is what binds them together and asks their help in the destruction of the harvest. All promise to cooperate, but immediately they hear the hymn "Glory to God in the Highest," that is, the wheat is being born (v. 1434). At this time, Night gives them the tools necessary to ruin the wheat and they set out.

The scene shifts again to Talent, Thought, and Time, as the first two wonder what the harmonious song "Glory to God" means. Again, they turn to Time for an answer. Talent has seen everything that has happened thus far but still does not understand how the life of the wheat can be compared with Christ's life (vv. 1528–30). That, Time answers, will be a matter of waiting and watching; Faith will do the rest. While Talent still suffers from confused doubts, Thought comes running with the news that the foremen of the two groups have finished the work and are on their way to Bethlehem, singing and dancing.

Night reappears, hidden among the groups, to inspect the success of his three helpers. Idolatry, Judaism, and Apostasy, arriving at Bethlehem, are unimpressed by the building, practically in ruins, inside which a Young Man is lying down. Grace tells the laborers to offer him the sheafs they brought. When they ask why, Grace answers that now Talent may be able to learn Time's lesson by seeing before him the Young Man prefigured in the wheat offered to him. He will consecrate it, and the element that was mere bread becomes flesh. This is too difficult for them to accept, but Talent says that faith will make it easy (v. 1666).

They inquire of the Young Man who he is. He is He who is:

He is God's Son. Having come to take back to God a sample of the fruits of the harvest, He took refuge in this inn to protect Himself from the storm caused by Night. The three enemies refuse to believe much of it. Idolatry cannot accept that God is the only ruler of Time and he threatens to eradicate the wheat with his sickle or to stain the sickle with His blood so that He may die as wheat, since He is born as wheat (vv. 1725–26). Judaism cannot believe that He is God's Son, and threatens to grind Him so that He may die like wheat, since He is born like it. Apostasy, in turn, cannot accept that bread can be changed into flesh, but hopes he will not have to use the tips of his winnowing fork to nail Him and raise Him for He will suffer like wheat, because He was born like wheat (vv. 1779–80). The enemies leave while Night and Talent remain. Night insinuates that Talent's difficulties with the meaning of the texts amount to sins because they deal with matters of faith, but the latter denies that this is true; he is trying to reconcile the two texts, for his faith is firm and unwavering (vv. 1819–20). Calderón thus indicates that there is nothing wrong in illuminating one point of faith with examples from other areas: he is not questioning the truth of faith, but trying to illuminate it.

Night argues with Talent about the validity of comparing the wheat to the Young Man in a passage of swift dialogue. The debate leads naturally to the last moments in the life of the wheat and of Christ. Night recognizing that Talent has won the argument, is desperate and would kill Talent as a way of preventing others from believing the same. As Night runs after Talent, a Young Man stops her. She calls on Idolatry who would cut him down with his scythe yet cannot. Night calls on Apostasy who attempts to nail Him but cannot. Lastly, she calls on Judaism, who kills Him with a cross (v. 1973+), then flees, realizing the enormity of his crime.

Night falls after the Young Man's death, the Night of Nights of the Day of Days: the end of the world. Time summons all the laborers to give them their salary as the trumpet of judgment sounds; Night will be the prosecutor. Time asks Talent whether he has any more doubts. He still has one left: why is it necessary to die in order to be born again (vv. 2125–26)? Saying that the answer is forthcoming, Time calls each group.

As Natural Law affirms that her group prepared the land, one of the carts opens and shows "a young girl, representing the Virgin" (v. 2142+). Pleased, Time gives her five talents.

Written Law took care of the wheat. In a second cart, a Nativity scene appears (v. 2176+). When Time asks Judaism what he did with the wheat, the latter claims he cut it, thrashed it, and ground it. Time disapproves but exempts Moses and those of his followers who go on to the Law of Grace. Night inquires who is the Law of Grace. Time answers: the one who gathered the grain which the cruel Hebrews put to death and which now faith multiplies, turning it into bread. Once the wheat died on the ground, it gave fruit which is the glory of heaven (vv. 2207–12). Night has one more question: who assures us of all this? The answer comes from the Young Man standing by the Blessed Sacrament in another cart: "I do, for being born again like the grain of wheat which died on the ground and produced a hundredfold, I put in this white bread My body and My soul. In it man has nourishment for his body and soul" (vv. 2213–21). Time asks one final time if Talent has any more doubts: He does not. The play ends with a musical invitation to come and see that the bread of this wheat is truly the bread of angels (the Eucharist) (vv. 2232–35).

In this *auto* Calderón explains how he proceeded in writing a sacramental play. A play begins to form when Talent, thas is, the human mind comes across two statements about the same thing which seem at first sight irreconcilable. This fact whets Talent's curiosity. Is he able to adjust the apparent contradiction in the statements? Talent turns for help to Thought who suggests going to Time, a personality truly multifaceted. First of all, he represents history and, more specifically, sacred history. Second, since sacred history is the manifestation of God's providence to us, Time can be called a paterfamilias, God's representative (*alcalde*), head shepherd, and even God's secondary cause. Calderón turns to sacred history and not to dogmatic theology to explain the meaning of the mystery of the Eucharist.

Sacred history can be conveniently divided into various stages poetically comparable to those which obtain in the cultivation of wheat. Since, as the title of the play indicates, sacred history can be compared to one single day, Calderón makes good use here of Christ's parable of the laborers in the vineyard wherein the day is divided into different parts, and groups of laborers are sent to the field at progressively later hours. In the present *auto* the vineyard is conveniently changed into a field of wheat because the play concerns the Eucharist. The parable of the vineyard provides another important element: The salary of the laborers depends not on the time spent on the field but on their attitude toward the harvest, that is, the Eucharist.

The parable of the vineyard is not the only source incorporated in this *auto*. The text that incited Talent's curiosity was "unless a wheat grain falls on the ground and dies, it remains only a single grain" (John 12:24). This statement is not part of any parable. Now the word wheat suggests sowing and field laborers. So Calderón uses the parable of the sower (Matt. 13:4–9,18–23) and also the story of the vineyard laborers (Matt. 20:1–16). To express the reward given to the laborers, Calderón turns to the parable of the talents (Matt. 25: 14–30). This *auto*, therefore exemplifies Calderón's effectiveness in providing unity to material taken from different sources and accommodating it to the allegory at hand. The variety of meanings of one single word sometimes provides links between different topics. For instance, the seed of the parable of the sower, as interpreted by Christ Himself, is the word (teachings) of God. We know that St. John calls Christ the Word (Son) of God (John 1:1). Consequently, speaking poetically, it is perfectly legitimate to equate the seed of the sower with Christ. Calderón is well supported here by a long exegetical tradition. In this *auto* Calderón presents sacred history from the Fall to Judgment as a series of concentric circles with the Eucharist as the innermost. All the others receive their meaning from it: the Mass, the feast of Corpus, the liturgical year, the life of each individual, and salvation history as a whole.

In my opinion the play succeeds magnifcently in showing us how the dramatist's mind wrestles with and solves the difficulties of fashioning an allegorical work, simultaneously creating a tense climate of suspense which constantly maintains the audience's attention. Finally, he manages to bring the play to a very satisfying conclusion. The end product is an impressive allegory, extremely rich in meaning and clear in content, although necessarily complicated in its presentation. This is so because what we are observing on stage is, if I may express it this way, not the play per se but the dramatist's mind in the process of organizing the materials he is to include in the play yet to be written. Due to Calderón's mastery in writing an *auto* about the process of writing an *auto*, we have an eloquent testimony of the playwright's confidence in his art; also, of the originality he often brought to it.

### Calderón's Contemporaries and Imitators

A few playwrights who were contemporaries of Calderón and others who came later wrote some *autos* which deserve to be mentioned. Francisco de Rojas Zorrilla (1607–1648), the author of perhaps nine *autos* and seemingly as ill at ease in this genre as was Tirso de Molina, nonetheless deserves some praise for two: *Naboth's Vineyard* (*La Viña de Nabot*) and *The Palace's Great Courtyard* (*El Gran Patio de Palacio*), which merit attention both for their competent treatment of the eucharistic theme and the allegorical technique. When reading Rojas's religious works one has the impression that his failure with the *autos* is likely due to a lack of deep religious conviction as well as his unfamiliarity with the technique of these works. Mac-Curdy says that "Rojas had neither the head nor the heart for writing *autos*. . . . he lacked knowledge and control of dogmatic theology. He had little feeling for liturgy and was not at ease working with allegory. . . . In short, Rojas' *autos* are deficient in content and form."[24]

Agustín Moreto y Cavana (1618–1669), like Rojas, owes his fame to his secular comedies. Four of his religious plays are extant, but only one *auto*, *The Great House of Austria and The Divine Margarita* (*La Gran Casa de Austria y Divina Margarita*). Reynolds has recently discovered Moreto's source, another *auto* by Mira de Amescua called *The Faith of Hungary* (*Le Fe de Hungría*).[25] Although Moreto's play is artistically superior to Mira's, both *autos* are somewhat marred by their primarily propagandistic intent.[26]

Francisco Bances Candamo (1662–1704) was a wholehearted admirer of Calderón and a great defender of the theater, strongly opposed to the growing attacks leveled against it. He wrote only three *autos*. One, *The First Duel of the World* (*El Primer Duelo del Mundo*) is closer to a cloak and dagger theme than to a sacramental play. The other two, *The Tables of Fortune* (*Las Mesas de la Fortuna*) and *The Great Chemist of the World* (*El Gran Químico del Mundo*) are not without some moments of excellent poetry, but their overcomplicated plots, inflated rhetoric, and distracting erudition point to a serious lack of poetic sincerity and true dramatic inspiration.[27]

The situation of the *auto* had become very critical by the middle of the eighteenth century, as influential Spanish intellectuals and literary critics became convinced admirers of French neoclassical ideas. For them the *autos sacramentales* were a totally unacceptable literary form. *Autos* not only dispensed with every aspect of verisimilitude, the form was felt to be filled with irreverence and profanity. As Clavijo y Fajardo put it in 1762, "if someone attempts to use the theater to present the teachings of Christianity for the purpose of our instruction, these teachings become ridiculous and a sign of ignorance; if they are presented for our entertainment, that is tantamount to irreverent boldness, reckless and scandalous." Clavijo exclaimed sorrowfully: "It really seems incredible that such a Christian nation can witness without horror the mysteries of its religion being thus profaned."[28] As Parker says, Clavijo "is not anxious for reform, only for abolition."[29] These groundless and unfair attacks remained without an adequate response, for no playwrights of stature were cultivating the genre. The weak attempts to defend the *autos* made by some critics were no match to the objections raised by Nasarre, Clavijo, and Moratín; and in 1765 King Charles III proclaimed a decree "prohibiting in the most absolute way performances of the *autos* despite the tremendous popularity these plays still enjoyed among the people."[30]

CHAPTER 7

# Summation

IN the preceding pages, I endeavored first to provide the
reader with the necessary information on the feast of Corpus
Christi, the liturgy in general, some literary manifestations with
the Eucharist as theme, and the Spanish dramatic tradition
before the *auto*. An understanding of these factors makes the
appearance and content of the sacramental plays less of an
enigma. Second, I tried to trace the development of the *auto*
to its demise, concentrating on those authors and works considered significant for their aesthetic value or for the new elements with which they enriched the genre.

Now, at the end of this study, I ask the reader to consider
my tentative conclusions, applicable to the genre as a whole.
Every critic knows that it is practically impossible to realize
fully what a given work means to its author or his contemporaries. But the critic also knows that through diligent and
sympathetic study one can arrive at a formulation of certain
guidelines useful in the interpretation of literary works or periods. Although the *autos* were written by many authors and
in different literary times, they show, in my opinion, a remark-
able number of common characteristics. Not all of them are
realized in the same degree in every sacramental play. The
reader should accept these characteristics as helpful suggestions,
not as rigid or inflexible rules. Following are those elements
which I consider most important:

1. The *autos* present a consistent world view and philosophy
of life—the Catholic world view. It is based upon and derived
from the history of salvation as it appears primarily in the Bible.
The salient points of this history are: (*a*) the existence before
time of the Trinity (Father, Son, and Holy Spirit), who create
the angels; (*b*) the rebellion of the bad angels and the begin-

ning of the rivalry between good and evil; (c) the Creation in time of the world and man; (d) the Fall of man; (e) the Redemption by Christ; (f) the founding of the Church; and (g) the end of the world with the punishment of the bad and the reward of the good.

2. God is the main agent in sacred history. He creates out of love and for a purpose. But this purpose cannot be realized without the cooperation of the free beings He has created. Some oppose this purpose—the devils and evil men; others favor it—the angels and good men. By choosing one or the other, each free being determines his final fate.

3. Sacred history, with God as its main agent, is also the gradual revelation of God's will and purpose. This revelation is made through men in human fashion, that is, taking into consideration the human condition. It follows the pedagogical principle of going from the simple to the complex, from shadows to light, from appearance to reality. Each stage is intimately united to the previous and successive ones, being in a way a fulfillment of the preceding stages and, at the same time, a sketch and sign of future, clearer realities. This process will ultimately end with God's final revelation to us in the afterlife.

4. An important consequence of the nature of this process is the fact that men and events, even though they are real and historical, become signs and symbols of something else. The language of signs—metaphorical language—is the proper means of expressing these relationships and realities. For this reason, God's revelation lends itself naturally to poetic treatment. In the poetic treatment of divine revelation, the playwright enjoys the freedom of expression proper to poetry, perhaps less precise conceptually than the language of analogy used in theology, but equally legitimate and valid. The *autos*, then, are dramatic renditions of some aspects of divine revelation.

5. In sacred history, the Eucharist is the sign par excellence of God's plan for us. Like all signs, the Eucharist tends toward something else as toward its fulfillment. The *autos* constantly express this tension toward a final fulfillment which will take place outside of time and which is symbolized in the eucharistic banquet. The usual trajectory of the *autos*, parallelling that of sacred history, is one which goes from a state of doubt to a

state of illumination. A similar movement often exists in secular plays also, but in these plays it does not transcend the human context.

6. Divine revelation ultimately makes sense only to the man of faith. The *autos* presuppose this acceptance of faith. The didactic element so pervasive and important in them does not aim at convincing those without faith but at illuminating and reviving a faith already existing. It is absolutely necessary to remember this fact if one wants to understand the dynamics of the *autos*. They do not obey the principle of casuality as we ordinarily understand it, but follow the logic of faith, valid only to the believer. This logic is not based on data collected by our senses or on the discursive power of reason left to itself.

7. The object of the *autos* is to teach moral doctrine, immediately applicable to the conduct of the individual, not abstract ideas. The *autos* aim at moving the will to action rather than at satisfying the intellect or at assuaging man's emotions by means of a cathartic experience. The final scenes are an invitation to worship, understood as religious behavior.

Let me conclude by expressing the hope that the present volume may help to foster the interest of a wider reading public in this most Spanish literary form, so universal in the dramatization of themes.

# Notes and References

## Preface

1. Jean-Louis Flecniakoska, *La formation de l' "auto" religieux en Espagne avant Calderón (1550–1635)* (Montpellier, 1961), pp. 15–82. Hereafter referred to as Flecniakoska and included in the text when it is the only source quoted. All translations from foreign languages throughout this volume are mine.
2. Bruce W. Wardropper, *Introducción al teatro religioso del siglo de oro. Evolución del auto sacramental antes de Calderón.* 2nd ed. (Salamanca, 1967), pp. 27–37. Hereafter referred to as Wardropper and included in the text when it is the only source quoted.
3. Pedro Calderón de la Barca, *Obras completas. Tomo III. Autos sacramentales.* Recopilación, prólogo y notas por Angel Valbuena Prat, 2nd ed. (Madrid, 1967), p. 427.

## Chapter One

1. Cyrille Lambot, "L'office de la Fête-Dieu. Aperçus nouveaux sur ses origines," *Revue Bénédictine*, 54 (1942), pp. 61–123. Provides an excellent introduction to the origins of the feast and the liturgy of Corpus. See also L. M. J. Delaissé, "A la recherche des origines de l'office du Corpus Christi dans les mss. liturgiques," *Scriptorium*, 4 (1950), pp. 220–39.
2. All the important documents relating to the feast of Corpus can be found in Peter Browe, *Textus antiqui de festo Corporis Christi* (Münster in Westfalien, 1934), in Cyrille Lambot and I. Fransen, *L'office de la Fête-Dieu primitive.* Textes et mélodies retrouvés (Maredsous, 1946). There is a very interesting fifteenth century Spanish translation of some readings of the office bearing the title *Estoria de la fiesta del Cuerpo de Dios* and included in *El espéculo de los legos.* Texto inédito del siglo XV. Ed., est., y notas por José Ma. Mohedano Hernández (Madrid, 1951), pp. 467–80.
3. For the Divine Office of Corpus Christi, I have consulted the *Roman Breviary* and the *Roman Missal.*
4. Cyprian Vagaggini, O. S B., *Theological Dimensions of the Liturgy.* A General Treatise on the Theology of the Liturgy. Trans.

by L. J. Doyle and W. A. Jurgens (Collegeville, Minn., 1976), p. 27. Hereafter referred to as Vagaggini and included in the text when it is the only source quoted.

5. The phrase is St. Augustine's, *Sermon* 272. He is quoted by Vagaggini, p. 43.

6. Sister Teresa Clare Goode, *Gonzalo de Berceo. El sacrificio de la Misa.* A Study of Its Symbolism and of Its Sources (Washington, D.C., 1933).

7. Luis Maldonado, *La plegaria eucarística.* Estudio de teología bíblica y litúrgica sobre la Misa (Madrid, 1967), p. 245 ff.

8. Vagaggini, p. 104; L. Maldonado, *La plegaria,* p. 106 ff.

9. Vagaggini, p. 111; L. Maldonado, *La plegaria,* p. 498.

10. On the prophetic value of the Eucharist, see Alfredo Sáenz, S. J., "El futuro: tensión hacia la gloria del cielo," *Estudios* (B. Aires), No. 558 (1964), pp. 570–579, and L. Maldonado, *La plegaria,* pp. 268–69.

11. The role of the Devil in the *autos* and other plays of the Spanish Golden Age has been the subject of important recent studies. See Alexander A. Parker, *The Theology of the Devil in the Drama of Calderón* (London, 1958), included also in *Critical Essays on the Theater of Calderón,* ed. Bruce W. Wardropper, (New York, 1965), pp. 3–23, with the title *The Devil in the Drama of Calderón.* Also J.-L. Flecniakoska, "Les rôles de Satan dans les pièces du *Códice de autos viejos," Revue des Langues Romanes* (Montpellier), 75 (1963), pp. 195–207, and his "Les rôles de Satan dans les autos de Lope de Vega," *Bulletin Hispanique,* 66 (1964), pp. 30–44; Angel L. Cilveti, *El demonio en el teatro de Calderón* (Valencia, 1977); Louise Fothergill-Payne, *La alegoría en los autos y farsas anteriores a Calderón* (London, 1977), pp. 118–48.

12. Flecniakoska, p. 442; L. Fothergill-Payne, *La alegoría,* p. 46.

13. William J. Entwistle exaggerates the polemic aspect of Calderón's *autos* in "La controversia en los autos de Calderón," *Nueva Revista de Filología Hispánica,* 2 (1948), pp. 223–38.

14. Wardropper, p. 116; Flecniakoska, pp. 393–427.

15. Francis George Very, *The Spanish Corpus Christi Procession: A Literary and Folkloric Study* (Valencia, 1962). Hereafter referred to as Very and included in the text when it is the only source quoted.

16. J. Romeu Figueras, "Notas al aspecto dramático de la procesión del Corpus en Cataluña," *Estudios Escénicos* (Barcelona), 1 (1957), pp. 32–33.

17. *Ibid.,* pp. 37–39.

18. Fernando Lázaro Carreter, ed., *Teatro medieval*, 2nd ed. (Madrid, 1965), p. 51.

19. Carmen Torroja Menéndez and María Rivas Palá, *Teatro en Toledo en el siglo XV*. "*Auto de la pasión*" *de Alonso del Campo* (Madrid, 1977), pp. 12–14.

20. *Ibid.*, p. 20.

21. *Ibid.*, pp. 24–29.

22. *Ibid.*, p. 29.

23. *Ibid.*, p. 26.

24. *Ibid.*, pp. 40–44, for a complete description of the procession at Toledo towards the end of the fifteenth century.

25. *Ibid.*, p. 44. On pp. 46–47, there is an extremely interesting chronological table of the *autos* staged from 1493 to 1510.

26. Vicente Lleó Cañal, *Arte y espectáculo: la fiesta del Corpus Christi en Sevilla en los siglos XVI y XVII* (Sevilla, 1975), p. 48.

27. A description of the *tarasca* is given here later on pp. 36–37. J. E. Varey includes reproductions of nine *tarascas* in his *Historia de los títeres en España (desde sus orígenes hasta mediados del siglo XVIII)* (Madrid, 1975), pp. 480–88.

28. Very, p. 16; V. Lleó Cañal, *Arte*, p. 50.

29. Jean-Louis Flecniakoska, "Les fêtes du Corpus a Ségovie (1594–1636). Documents inédits," *Bulletin Hispanique*, 56 (1954), pp. 28–242.

30. Fray Luis de Granada, *Obras* III (Madrid, 1945), p. 22 ff.

31. The poem is found in *Romancero y cancionero sagrados* (Madrid, 1950), p. 545.

32. Pedro Calderón de la Barca, *Obras*, III, p. 1726.

## Chapter Two

1. B. W. Wardropper has a whole chapter on the public attending the *autos* in his *Introducción*, pp. 85–95.

2. Antonio Martí, *La preceptiva retórica española en el Siglo de Oro* (Madrid, 1972) is an excellent study with very good bibliography.

3. Melquíades Andrés, *La teología española en el siglo XVI*, 2 vols. (Madrid, 1976), I, p. 312; II, pp. 635–36.

4. Fray Dionisio Vázquez, *Sermones*. Prólogo y notas del P. Félix G. Olmedo, S. J. (Madrid, 1956), pp. XLII, LIV–LV.

5. It is a *Sermon on the Resurrection* and the complete text can be found on pp. 3–43 of source, cited in note 4. I have indicated the page after the quotation in the text.

6. The text of the sermon can be found in Fray Luis de Granada, *Obras*, III, pp. 22–25. Pages are given in the text.

7. Ada Marshall Johnson, *Hispanic Silverwork* (New York, 1944), p. 22.

8. José Camón Aznar, *La arquitectura y la orfebrería españolas del siglo XVI* (Madrid, 1959), p. 507.

9. The title reads *Descripción de la traça y ornato de la Custodia de plata de la Sancta Iglesia de Sevilla*. There is a reprint in Seville, 1887. Pages are given in the text.

10. For information on other monstrances and Spanish silverwork, see Anselmo Gascón de Gotor, *El Corpus Christi y las custodias procesionales de España* (Barcelona, 1916); Charles Oman, *The Golden Age of Hispanic Silver, 1400–1665* (London, 1968).

11. Quoted in M. Menéndez Pelayo, *Antología de poetas líricos castellanos*, III (Madrid, 1944), p. 74.

12. Marcel Bataillon, "Chanson pieuse et poésie de devotion," *Bulletin Hispanique*, 27 (1925), pp. 231–32.

13. *Ibid.*, p. 232.

14. The text is found in *Romancero*, pp. 401–7.

15. *Ibid.*, p. 404 a.

16. *Ibid.*, p. 462 a.

17. The *loa*, alone or together with an *introito*, was an introduction to the play. See Joseph A. Meredith, *Introito and loa in the Spanish Drama of the Sixteenth Century* (Philadelphia, 1908), and the more recent, J.-L. Flecniakoska, *La loa* (Madrid, 1975).

18. *Romancero*, p. 545 b.

19. Bruce W. Wardropper, *Historia de la poesía lírica a lo divino en la cristiandad occidental* (Madrid, 1958).

20. Wardropper, pp. 131–147, and Flecniakoska, pp. 159–223.

21. José Ramón Guerrero, *Catecismos españoles del siglo XVI* (Madrid, 1969), pp. 148–259; M. Andrés, *La teología*, I, p. 267.

22. M. Bataillon, *Erasmo y España*. Trad. de A. Alatorre (México, 1966), pp. 210, 560; M. Andrés, *La teología*, II, pp. 143–147.

23. M. Bataillon, *Erasmo*, pp. 214, 538; Fray Domingo de Valtanás, O.P., *Apologías* (Barcelona, 1963), has a defense of frequent communion (*Apología de la frecuentación de la sacrosanta eucharistía y comunión*) on pp. 191–213.

24. For complete information on these questions see J. Beguiristain, *Rectificaciones históricas sobre la comunión frecuente y diaria en España* (Buenos Aires, 1922), and Jac. Nouwens, "Los autores españoles y la disputa de la comunión frecuente en los Países Bajos," *Analecta Sacra Tarraconensia*, 25 (1952), pp. 221–54.

## Chapter Three

1. Representative of the first group would be Humberto López Morales, *Tradición y creación en los orígenes del teatro castellano* (Madrid, 1968), and his "Nueva hipótesis sobre el teatro medieval castellano," *Revista de Estudios Hispánicos* (P. Rico), 2 (1972), pp. 7–19. Critics with a different point of view are F. Lázaro Carreter, ed., *Teatro*, and especially Charlotte Stern, "The *Coplas de Mingo Revulgo* and the Early Spanish Drama," *Hispanic Review*, 44 (1976), pp. 311–32, with bibliography of her previous studies; and José M. Regueiro, "Rito y popularismo en el teatro antiguo español," *Romanische Forschungen*, 89 (1977), pp. 1–17.

2. J. M. Regueiro, "Rito," p. 8.

3. O. B. Hardison, Jr., *Christian Rite and Christian Drama in the Middle Ages*, (Baltimore, 1965), p. 285.

4. F. Lázaro Carreter, ed., *Teatro*, pp. 37–45; J. E. Varey, "A Note on the Councils of the Church and Early Dramatic Spectacles in Spain," in *Medieval Hispanic Studies Presented to Rita Hamilton*, ed. A. D. Deyermond (London, 1976), p. 244.

5. F. Lázaro Carreter, ed., *Teatro*, p. 49; J. Romeu Figueras, "Notas," p. 36.

6. Alexander A. Parker, "Notes on the Religious Drama in Medieval Spain and the Origins of the *Auto Sacramental.*" *Modern Language Review*, 30 (1935), p. 172.

7. F. Lázaro Carreter, ed., *Teatro*, p. 48.

8. *Ibid.*, p. 50.

9. Wardropper, p. 57.

10. C. Torroja Menéndez and M. Rivas Palá, *Teatro en Toledo*, p. 20.

11. *Ibid.*, pp. 28–29.

12. *Ibid.*, pp. 46–47.

13. A. A. Parker, "Notes," p. 177.

14. *Ibid.*, p. 178.

15. *Ibid.*

16. F. Lázaro Carreter, ed., *Teatro*, p. 55.

17. A. A. Parker, "Notes," p. 178.

18. F. Lázaro Carreter, ed., *Teatro*, pp. 56–57, n. 10.

19. Emilio Cotarelo y Mori, "El primer auto sacramental del teatro español y noticia de su autor el Bachiller Hernán López de Yanguas," *Revista de Archivos, Bibliotecas y Museos*, 7 (1902), pp. 251–272.

20. A. A. Parker, "Notes," p. 180, n. 2.

21. *Teatro*, p. 51.

22. Alan H. Nelson, *The Medieval English Stage. Corpus Christi Pageants and Plays* (Chicago, 1974), pp. 2–5. Here he opposes Kolve's theories.

23. See note 1 of this chapter for her articles on Mingo Revulgo; C. Stern, "Fray Iñigo de Mendoza and Medieval Dramatic Ritual," *Hispanic Review*, 33 (1965), pp. 197–245. Julio Rodríguez-Puértolas, *Fray Iñigo de Mendoza y sus "Coplas de Vita Christi"* (Madrid, 1968), with the text of the *Coplas* on pp. 291–513.

24. C. Stern, "Las *Coplas*," p. 330.

25. C. Stern, "Fray Iñigo," p. 198.

26. *Ibid.*, p. 200.

27. C. Stern, "Some New Thoughts on the Early Spanish Drama," *Bulletin of the Comediantes*, 18 (1966), p. 15.

28. *Ibid.*, p. 16.

29. *Ibid.*, p. 18. See also her more recent study "The Early Spanish Drama: From Medieval Ritual to Renaissance Art," *Renaissance Drama*, 6 (1973), pp. 177–201.

30. A. A. Parker, "Notes," p. 180.

31. C. Torroja Menéndez and M. Rivas Palá, *Teatro en Toledo, passim.*

32. F. Lázaro Carreter, ed., *Teatro*, pp. 58–67.

33. See Georges Cirot, "Le théatre religieux d'Encina," *Bulletin Hispanique*, 43 (1941), pp. 5–35, and his "A propos d'Encina. Coup d'oeil sur notre vieux drame religieux," *Ibid.*, pp. 123–51; Wardropper, pp. 163–69; and the more recent and comprehensive study by Henry W. Sullivan, *Juan del Encina* (Boston, 1976).

34. Alfredo Hermenegildo, *Renacimiento, teatro y sociedad. Vida y obra de Lucas Fernández* (Madrid, 1975), p. 31; John Lihani, *Lucas Fernández* (New York, 1973), p. 54 ff.

35. A. Hermenegildo, *Renacimiento*, p. 32.

36. *Ibid.*, p. 80; J. Lihani, *Lucas Fernández*, pp, 54–62.

37. A. Hermenegildo, *Renacimiento*, p. 80; J. Lihani, *Lucas Fernández*, p. 100.

38. A. Hermenegildo, *Renacimiento*, p. 188.

39. They are found in verses 339–344. I used J. Lihani's edition of Lucas Fernández, *Farsas y églogas* (New York, 1969), pp. 129–130.

40. A. Hermenegildo, *Renacimiento*, pp. 212–13.

41. J. P. Migne, *Patrologia Latina*, vol. LXXXV, col. 419.

42. A. Hermenegildo, *Renacimiento*, p. 27; Jack Horace Parker, *Gil Vicente* (New York, 1967), pp. 24, 28.

43. J. H. Parker, *Gil Vicente*, p. 147.

44. M. Andrés, *La teología*, II, p. 5.

45. Aurelio Prudencio, *Obras completas en latín y castellano* (Madrid, 1950), p. 72*; M. Bataillon, *Erasmo*, pp. 15, 27, 273 y; Louise Fothergill-Payne, "La *Psychomachia* de Prudencio y el teatro alegórico pre-calderoniano," *Neophilologus*, 59 (1975), pp. 48–62.

46. M. Andrés, *La teología*, II, p. 62.

47. L. Fothergill-Payne, "La *Psychomachia*," p. 48; Aurelio Prudencio, *Obras*, p. 72*.

48. L. Fothergill-Payne, "La *Psychomachia*," p. 48.

49. M. Andrés, *La teología*, II, p. 61.

## Chapter Four

1. Fernán López de Yanguas, *Obras dramáticas*. Ed., estudio preliminar y notas de Fernando González Ollé (Madrid, 1967), p. XII.

2. L. Fothergill-Payne, *La alegoría*, pp. 46–48, 79.

3. Fernando González Ollé, "La *Farsa del Santísimo Sacramento*, anónima, y su significado en el desarrollo del auto sacramental," *Revista de Literatura*, 35 (1969), p. 135.

4. See his article cited in note 19 to chapter three. The play is included in F. López de Yanguas, *Obras*, pp. 127–34.

5. The quote is from Cotarelo's summary of the play. See *ibid.*, p. 131.

6. F. López de Yanguas, *Obras*, p. XXXVII.

7. *Ibid.*, p. XLII, and his "La *Farsa*," pp. 129–30.

8. F. González Ollé, "La *Farsa*," p. 129.

9. Diego Sánchez de Badajoz, *Recopilación en metro (Sevilla, 1554)*. Trabajo de seminario bajo la dirección de Frida Weber de Kurlat (Buenos Aires, 1968), p. 45.

10. *Ibid.*, pp. 49–50.

11. *Ibid.*, pp. 176–81, verses 301–536 of *The Play of Solomon* (*Farça de Salomón*).

12. J. López Prudencio, *Diego Sánchez de Badajoz. Estudio crítico, biográfico y bibliográfico* (Madrid, 1915), p. 122.

13. J. P. Wickersham Crawford, *Spanish Drama Before Lope de Vega* (Philadelphia, rpt. 1967), pp. 40–43.

14. D. Sánchez de Badajoz, *Recopilación*, p. 309.

15. Celina Sabor de Cortázar, "Un tema teológico en Diego Sánchez de Badajoz: las potencias del alma y su acción recíproca," in *Studia Hispanica in Honorem R. Lapesa*, II (Madrid, 1974), p. 556.

16. *Ibid.*, p. 557. The original plan of the *Recopilación* included

some of his sermons; see D. Sánchez de Badajoz, *Recopilación*, p. 47.

17. *Ibid.*, p. 575.

18. Jean-Louis Flecniakoska, "Vestiaire, accesoires, mise en scène et jeux scéniques dans le théatre de Diego Sánchez de Badajoz," in *Mélanges de langue et de littérature médiévales offerts à Pierre Le Gentile*, eds. Jean Dufournet and Daniel Poirion (Paris, 1973), p. 246.

19. *Ibid.*, pp. 254–55. See also N. D. Shergold, *A History of the Spanish Stage from Medieval Times Until the End of the Seventeenth Century* (Oxford, 1967), pp. 87–89.

20. See J. A. Meredith's chapter "The Didactic Introito in Sánchez de Badajoz and Others" in his *Introito and Loa*, pp. 57–80, and Donna J. Gustafson, "The Role of the Shepherd in the Pre-Lopean Drama of Diego Sánchez de Badajoz," *Bulletin of the Comediantes*, 25 (1973), pp. 5–13.

21. In D. Sánchez de Badajoz, *Recopilación*, pp. 393–402.

22. On the importance of man's faculties and senses in the sacramental plays, see L. Fothergill-Payne's chapter "Las tres potencias y los cinco sentidos" in her *La alegoría*, pp. 149–69.

23. See note 5 to chapter one. Isidore of Seville defines it in a similar way: *aliud enim sonat, aliud intelligitur* (*Etimologiae*, I, pp. 37, 22), and Angus Fletcher says: "In the simplest terms, allegory says one thing and means another," from *Allegory. The theory of a Symbolic Mode* (Ithaca, N.Y., 1964), p. 2.

24. See S. Sandmel, *Philo's Place in Judaism* (Cincinnati, 1956), and Erich Auerbach, "Figura," in his *Scenes from the Drama of European Literature* (Gloucester, Mass., 1973), pp. 54–56.

25. Henri de Lubac, *Histoire et Esprit: L'Intelligence de l'Ecriture d'après Origène* (Paris, 1950), and R. P. C. Hanson, *Allegory and Event. A Study of the Sources and Significance of Origen's Interpretation of Scripture* (Richmond, Va., 1959).

26. Two excellent studies on how these doctrines have been applied are Jean Danielou's *Sacramentum Futuri. Etudes sur les origines de la typologie biblique* (Paris, 1950), and Henri de Lubac's *Exégèse médiéval, les quatre sens de l'Ecriture*, 4 vols. (Paris, 1959–1964). Also of interest, see Kenneth E. Trent, *Types of Christ in the Old Testament* (New York, 1960).

27. A good example of this tendency is the subject of Sister Teresa Clare Goode. *Gonzalo de Berceo*, cited in note 6 to chapter one. Also David William Foster, *Christian Allegory in Early Hispanic Poetry* (Lexington, Ky., 1970), pp. 34–45.

28. See David William Foster, "Calderón's *La torre de Babilonia* and Christian Allegory," *Criticism*, 9 (1967), pp. 142–54.

29. Frida Weber de Kurlat, *Lo cómico en el teatro de Fernán González de Eslava* (Buenos Aires, 1963), p. 13.

30. William Shaffer Jack, *The Early "Entremés" in Spain: The Rise of a Dramatic Form* (Philadelphia, 1923), p. 31. Also Eugenio Asensio, *Itinerario del entremés*, 2nd ed. (Madrid, 1971), pp. 24–40.

31. Léo Rouanet, ed., *Colección de autos, farsas y coloquios del siglo XVI*, 4 vols. (Barcelona-Madrid, 1901), I, p. XIII.

32. F. Lázaro Carreter, ed., *Teatro*, pp. 57–58; C. Torroja Menéndez and M. Rivas Palá, *Teatro en Toledo*, pp. 72–74.

33. See Arturo Graf's excellent study, "Il *mistero* e le prime forme dell' *auto sacro* in Ispagna," in his *Studii drammatici* (Roma, 1878), pp. 251–325.

34. The text in L. Rouanet, ed., *Colección*, I, pp. 169–81.

35. See C. Stern, "The Early Spanish Drama," for ideas applicable here.

36. The text in L. Rouanet, ed., *Colección*, III, pp. 212–28.

37. See L. Fothergill-Payne, *La alegoría*, p. 63.

38. J. M. Aicardo, "Autos anteriores a Lope," *Razón y Fe*, 6 (1903), p. 209.

39. The text in L. Rouanet, ed., *Colección*, III, pp. 346–80.

40. Verses 202–204. There is a pun here which appears in many *autos*, based on the Spanish word "yerros" which has a dual meaning: that is, irons (chains) and errors (sins). See L. Fothergill-Payne, *La alegoría*, pp. 35–37, on the meaning and transformations of State of Innocence.

41. J. M. Aicardo, "Autos anteriores a Lope," *Razón y Fe*, 7 (1903), p. 163. Calderon's auto, *Life Is a Dream*, should not be confused with his three-act secular play of the same title.

42. Jean-Louis Flecniakoska, "Les conflicts tragiques dans l'auto religieux précaldéronien," in *Le théatre tragique*, ed. Jean Jacquot (Paris, 1962), p. 107.

43. *Ibid.*, p. 109. See also his "Les rôles de Satan dans les pièces du *Códice de autos viejos*," *Revue des Langues Romanes*, 75 (1963), pp. 195–207.

44. L. Fothergill-Payne, *La alegoría*, pp. 118–48.

45. Ten have been published, as follows: three by Alice Bowdoin Kemp, ed., *Three Autos Sacramentales of 1590* (Toronto, 1936); four by Vera Helen Buck, ed., *Four Autos Sacramentales of 1590* (Iowa City, 1937); and four by Carl Allen Tyre, ed., *Religious Plays of 1590* (Iowa City, 1938).

46. Text in A. B. Kemp, ed., *Three Autos*, pp. 74–107.

47. *Ibid.*, pp. 17–22, discusses the sources. See also Ramón Menéndez Pidal, *Romancero hispánico. Teoría e historia*, 2 vols., 2nd ed. (Madrid, 1968), I, pp. 286–89.

48. R. Meméndez Pidal, *Romancero*, II, pp. 103–6.

49. A. B. Kemp, ed., *Three Autos*, p. 81, n. to vv. 228–242.

50. Text in V. H. Buck, ed., *Four Autos*, pp. 23–43. Her analysis is on pp. 9–13.

51. *Ibid.*, the text, pp. 44–61.

52. *Ibid.*, pp. 13–14.

53. *Ibid.*, p. 13.

54. *Ibid.*, text, pp. 62–79.

55. *Ibid.*, pp. 17–20.

56. *Ibid.*, p. 18.

57. Aurelio Prudencio, *Obras completas*, pp. 52*–64*; E. Male, *L'art religieux du XIVe siècle en France*, I (Paris, 1968), pp. 201–253. L. Fothergill-Payne, "La *Psychomachia*."

58. Chandler Rathfon Post, *Medieval Spanish Allegory* (Cambridge, Mass., 1915, rpt. 1971), and D. W. Foster, *Christian Allegory*.

59. See the recent study of Robert A. Potter, *The English Morality Play*. Origins, History and Influence of a Dramatic Tradition (Boston, 1975).

60. A. Fletcher, *Allegory*, p. 7.

61. Text in V. H. Buck, ed., *Four Autos*, pp. 80–98.

62. *Ibid.*, pp. 21–22.

63. L. Fothergill-Payne, *La alegoría*, pp. 57–58.

### Chapter Five

1. John J. Reynolds, *Juan Timoneda* (Boston, 1975), p. 83.

2. Eduardo González Pedroso, ed., *Autos sacramentales desde sus orígenes hasta fines del siglo XVII* (Madrid, 1952), pp. 76–77.

3. Félix G. Olmedo, "Un nuevo ternario de Juan Timoneda," *Razón y Fe*, 47 (1917), pp. 281–82.

4. *Ibid.*, p. 485. Also Pilar Delgado Barnes, "Contribución a la bibliografía de Juan de Timoneda," *Revista de Literatura*, 16 (1959), p. 27. On p. 34, Delgado mentions a *Quaderno espiritual* by Timoneda, published posthumously in 1597, where *The Lost Sheep* is also included. But no copies of this *Quaderno* have been found.

5. E. González Pedroso, ed., *Autos*, p. 77.

6. J. J. Reynolds, *Juan Timoneda*, pp. 83–84.

7. E. González Pedroso, ed., *Autos*, p. 89.

8. *Ibid.*, p. 95; Wardropper, pp. 261–67.

9. María del Pilar Aróstegui, "La dramaturgia de Juan Timoneda. Estado actual de la cuestión," *Boletín de la Biblioteca de Menéndez Pelayo,* 48 (1972), pp. 204–11.

10. The text in Ricardo Arias, ed., *Auto sacramentales,* I (México, 1977), pp. 109–29.

11. The play has been studied by Wardropper, pp. 271–273; J. J. Reynolds, *Juan Timoneda,* pp. 83–86; and by Donald Thaddeus Dietz, *The "Auto Sacramental" and the Parable in Spanish Golden Age Literature* (Chapel Hill, N.C., 1973), pp. 49–62.

12. J. J. Reynolds, *Juan Timoneda,* pp. 85–86.

13. Text in R. Arias, ed., *Autos,* I, pp. 143–52.

14. The text of *Pragmatic Sanction,* in L. Rouanet, ed., *Colección,* III, pp. 245–60.

15. J. J. Reynolds, *Juan Timoneda,* p. 92. On pp. 91–93, he gives a summary and evaluation of the play.

16. Text in R. Arias, ed., *Autos,* I, pp. 131–42. J. J. Reynolds, *Juan Timoneda,* pp. 88–90, gives a summary and evaluation of the play. See also Wardropper, pp. 261–67. The text of the source play, *Farsa del Sacramento de la Fuente de San Juan,* can be found in E. González Pedroso, ed., *Autos,* pp. 100–103, and a better one in L. Rouanet, ed., *Colección,* III, pp. 180–99.

17. D. T. Dietz, *The "Auto,"* pp. 137–61.

18. E. González Pedroso, ed., *Autos,* p. 106, b, n. 1.

19. D. T. Dietz, *The "Auto,"* p. 145.

20. *Ibid.,* p. 145.

21. See Wardropper, pp. 252–53; J. J. Reynolds, *Juan Timoneda,* pp. 11–14; F. G. Olmedo, "Un nuevo," p. 279.

22. Marcel Bataillon, "Ensayo de explicación del 'Auto sacramental'," en *Varia lección de clásicos españoles* (Madrid, 1964), pp. 188–91.

23. Américo Castro and Hugo H. Rennert, *Vida de Lope de Vega.* Adiciones de Fernando Lázaro Carreter (Salamanca, 1969), pp. 501–3; Flecniakoska, pp. 39–55.

24. Marcelino Menéndez Pelayo, *Estudios sobre el teatro de Lope de Vega* (Santander, 1949), I, p. 25.

25. *Ibid.,* p. 34.

26. S. Griswold Morley, "Strophes in the Spanish Drama Before Lope de Vega," *Homenaje ofrecido a Menéndez Pidal* (Madrid, 1925), I, pp. 505–31.

27. Dámaso Alonso has commented on the philosophical depth of Lope's poems in *Poesía española. Ensayo de métodos y límites estilísticos* (Madrid, 1950), pp. 487–97.

28. The text can be found in Lope de Vega, *Obras. VI. Autos y coloquios.* I. Ed. y estudio preliminar de M. Menéndez Pelayo (Madrid, 1963), pp. 269–86, and in Lope Félix de Vega Carpio, *Obras escogidas. III. Teatro* (Madrid, 1967), pp. 51–65. The page references in the text are from this edition.

29. Julio Rodríguez-Puértolas studies the presence of the theme of honor in Lope's plays in "La transposición de la realidad en los autos sacramentales de Lope de Vega," *Bulletin Hispanique,* 72 (1970), pp. 96–112. Also Bruce W. Wardropper, "Honor in the Sacramental Plays of Valdivielso and Lope de Vega," *Modern Language Notes,* 66 (1951), pp. 81–88. L. Fothergill-Payne, *La alegoría,* pp. 99–100.

30. Fray Modesto de Sanzoles, "La alegoría como constante estilística de Lope de Vega en los autos sacramentales," *Revista de Literatura,* 16 (1959), pp. 123–25.

31. Text in R. Arias, ed., *Autos,* I, pp. 177–99.

32. D. T. Dietz gives his own evaluation of this piece and a good summary of recent criticism in his book, *The "Auto,"* pp. 93–97. See also Fray M. de Sanzoles, "La alegoría," pp. 129–32, and L. Fothergill-Payne, *La alegoría,* p. 25.

33. The text is in Lope de Vega, *Obras. VI. Autos y coloquios. I.* pp. 105–21.

34. Bethlehem means the house of bread.

35. There are many references to the Devil's brand in the *autos.* It was usually represented by the letter S and the figure of a nail (*clavo*). Together they read slave (*es-clavo*).

36. M. Menéndez Pelayo, *Estudios,* I. p. 63; J. M. Aicardo, "Autos sacramentales de Lope," *Razón y Fe,* 21 (1908), pp. 447–48; Fray M. de Sanzoles, "La alegoría," pp. 125–127.

37. Flecniakoska, pp. 309, 311–312, 443; and J. Rodríguez-Puértolas, "La transposición, pp. 96–112.

38. Fray M. de Sanzoles, "La alegoría," pp. 115, 126.

39. J. M. Aicardo, "Autos sacramentales de Lope," *Razón y Fe,* 19 (1907), p. 459.

40. M. Menéndez Pelayo, *Estudios,* pp. 72, 82; Wardropper, p. 288; Fray M. de Sanzoles, "La alegoría," pp. 113–16.

41. *Ibid.,* pp. 124, 125, 129, 133.

42. Arturo M. Cayuela, "Los autos sacramentales de Lope, reflejo de la cultura religiosa del poeta y de su tiempo," *Razón y Fe,* 108 (1935), p. 170.

43. Poetry *a lo divino* is secular poems and songs which, through subtle changes in vocabulary, are given a new religious content. Val-

divielso's importance in this field has been studied by J. M. Aguirre, *José de Valdivielso y la poesía religiosa tradicional* (Toledo, 1965). Valdivielso's religious epic poems are discussed in Frank Pierce's *La poesía épica del Siglo de Oro*, 2nd ed. (Madrid, 1968), *passim*.

44. See Wardropper, p. 294, for Salas Barbadillo's high opinion of Valdivielso's *autos*. Vicente Espinel's assessment can be seen in José de Valdivielso. *Teatro Completo*. Ed. y notas de Ricardo Arias and Robert V. Piluso (Madrid, 1975), I, p. 24. References to above edition are given in parenthesis in the text.

45. Ricardo Arias, "Refranes y frases proverbiales en el teatro de Valdivielso," *Revista de Archivos, Bibliotecas y Museos*, LXXXI (1978), pp. 241–88.

46. D. T. Dietz, The *"Auto,"* pp. 44–49.

47. Wardropper, pp. 296, 299; D.T. Dietz, The *"Auto,"* pp. 44–48, 65–68; José de Valdivielso, *El hospital de los locos. La Serrana de Plasencia*, ed. J.-L. Flecniakoska (Salamanca, 1971), pp. 7–33.; R. Arias, *"El hospital de los locos*, de Valdivielso, interpretación dramática de la metáfora locura-pecado," in *Estudios de historia, literatura y arte hispánicos ofrecidos a Rodrigo A. Molina* (Madrid, 1977), pp. 25–37.

48. The text is in J. de Valdivielso, *Teatro Completo*, I, pp. 127–62.

49. L. Fothergill-Payne, *La alegoría*, pp. 155, 168. In Sánchez de Badajoz's *The Play of Isaac*, the fallibility of the senses was one of the main topics of the *auto*. See above, pp. 71–72.

50. George Camamis, *Estudios sobre el cautiverio en el Siglo de Oro* (Madrid, 1977).

51. The text is in J. de Valdivielso, *Teatro Completo*, I, pp. 513–51.

52. L. Fothergill-Payne, *La alegoría*, p. 74.

53. *Ibid.*, p. 198.

54. The red color is chosen because of a double meaning in Spanish: *encarnado* means red and also incarnate (made man).

55. For the complete list of Mira's plays, see Flecniakoska, pp. 64–71; James A. Castañeda, *Mira de Amescua* (Boston, 1977), pp. 147–64. On *Peter Telonario*, see A. Valbuena Prat's introduction to Antonio Mira de Amescua, *Teatro. I* (Madrid, 1943), and José María Bella, "Origen y difusión de la leyenda de Pedro Telonario y sus derivaciones en el teatro del Siglo de Oro, (Mira de Amescua y Felipe Godínez)," *Revista de Filología Española*, 55 (1972), pp. 51–59.

56. A. Mira de Amescua, *Teatro*, I, p. LXXV.

57. J.-L. Flecniakoska, "Las figuras de Herejía y Demonio al servicio de la propaganda política en los autos de Mira de Amescua," *Boletín de la Biblioteca de Menéndez Pelayo*, 52 (1976), p. 206.

58. *Ibid.*, p. 212.

59. *Ibid.*, p. 214.

60. *Ibid.*, p. 209.

61. Wardropper, p. 327; J. A. Castañeda, *Mira de Amescua*, pp. 140–42.

62. The text is in Tirso de Molina (Fray Gabriel Téllez), *Obras dramáticas completas*. Ed. crítica por Blanca de los Ríos I, 3 vols. (Madrid, 1946–1958), pp. 141–59. See also Flecniakoska, pp. 71–78, and Margaret Wilson, *Tirso de Molina* (Boston, 1977), pp. 126–29.

63. The text is in Tirso de Molina, *Obras*, I, pp. 549–65.

64. *Ibid.*, p. 635. Also L. Fothergill-Payne, *La alegoría*, pp. 96–98.

65. The text is in Tirso de Molina, *Obras*, I, pp. 1687–1705.

66. L. Fothergill-Payne, *La alegoría*, pp. 101–2.

67. The text is in T. de Molina, *Obras*, II, pp. 745–82.

68. *Ibid.*, the text III, pp. 1299–1317.

69. *Ibid.*, p. 1315.

70. *Ibid.*, p. 1317.

71. Serge Maurel, in *L'universe dramatique de Tirso de Molina* (Poitiers, 1971), p. 347, rightly says that "the allegory of the *auto* loses its abstract character in Tirso's theater. He resorts to images rather than to ideas; we can see him trying to present and make tangible the invisible part of our humanity, the hidden reality of the divine made-flesh." I cannot see, however, how this realistic tendency can be considered a positive element in allegory since this mode usually aims at the abstract and universal.

## Chapter Six

1. Margaret Wilson, *Spanish Drama of the Golden Age* (Oxford, 1969), p. 183.

2. A. Baumgartner, S. J., "Calderons Autos," *Stimmen aus Maria Laach*, 34 (1888), pp. 195–211; Angel Valbuena Prat, "Los autos sacramentales de Calderón (clasificación y análisis)," *Revue Hispanique*, 61 (1924), pp. 1–302; A. A. Parker, *The Allegorical*, p. 62.

3. *Ibid.*, p. 69.

4. See M. Andrés's two volume work *La teología española en el siglo XVI*.

5. M. Wilson, *Spanish Drama*, p. 153.

6. The statement is by Father Juan Ignacio Castroverde and is quoted by A. A. Parker, *The Allegorical*, p. 14.

7. José Ma. de Cossío, "Racionalismo del arte dramático de Calderón," *Cruz y Raya*, 21 (1934), pp. 37–76.

8. Everett W. Hesse, "La dialéctica y el casuismo en Calderón," *Estudios* (Madrid), 9 (1953), pp. 517–31.

9. Angel L. Cilveti, *El significado de "La vida es sueño"* (Valencia, 1971), pp. 225–27.

10. A. A. Parker, *The Allegorical*, pp. 72–90.

11. P. Calderón de la Barca, *Obras Completas. Tomo III. Autos sacramentales*, 2nd ed. Recopilación, prólogo y notas por A. Valbuena Prat (Madrid, 1967), p. 42.

12. Jack Sage, "Calderón y la música teatral," *Bulletin Hispanique*, 58 (1956), pp. 281–89.

13. *Ibid.*, p. 300. See also Alice M. Pollin, "*Cithara Iesu*: La apoteosis de la música en *El divino Orfeo* de Calderón," in *Homenaje a Casalduero: Crítica y poesía*, ed. Rizel Pincus Sigele and Gonzalo Sobejano (Madrid, 1972), pp. 419–31, and her "Calderón de la Barca and Music: Theory and Examples in the *Autos* (1675–1681)," *Hispanic Review*, 41 (1973), pp. 362–70.

14. N. D. Shergold, *A History*, pp. 452 ff.

15. Manuel Ruiz Lagos, "Las alegorías inanimadas como técnica escenográfica en el teatro simbólico de Calderón," *Archivum* (Oviedo), 15 (1965), pp. 256–74, and also his "Una técnica dramática de Calderón: la pintura y el centro escénico," *Segismundo*, 2 (1966), pp. 91–104.

16. Eunice Joiner Gates, "Calderón's Interest in Art," *Philological Quarterly*, 40 (1961), 53–67.

17. Emilio Orozco Díaz, *El teatro y la tetralidad del Barroco*, (Barcelona, 1969), p. 11. Of special interest here is Chapter V on the theatrical aspect of the theater itself.

18. I followed the text in my anthology, *Calderón de la Barca, Autos sacramentales* (México, 1978), I, pp. 213–61.

19. A. A. Parker, *The Allegorical*, p. 200. See also Pollin's article cited in note 13.

20. Jorge Páramo Pomareda, "Consideraciones sobre los 'autos mitológicos' de Calderón de la Barca," *Thesaurus* (Bogotá), 12 (1957), pp. 51–80.

21. On the role of music in this *auto*, see Pollin's article cited in note 13.

22. I followed the text in my anthology, *Calderón de la Barca, Autos*, pp. 367–423.

23. For the special place of this work in the development of Cal-

derón's theory of the *autos,* see A. A. Parker, *The Allegorical,* pp. 82–105.

24. Raymond R. MacCurdy, *Francisco de Rojas Zorilla* (New York, 1968), p. 93; also see his *Francisco de Rojas Zorrilla: bibliografía crítica* (Madrid, 1965), for complete bibliographical information.

25. John J. Reynolds, "The source of Moreto's only *Auto Sacramental,*" *Bulletin of the Comediantes,* 24 (1972), pp. 21–22.

26. For a summary of Moreto's *auto* see James A. Castañeda, *Agustín Moreto* (New York, 1974), pp. 109–110. A summary of the source play can be found in Castañeda's *Mira de Amescua* (Boston, 1977), pp. 149–51.

27. José J. Pérez Feliú, *Autos sacramentales de Fco. Bances Candamo* (Oviedo, 1975). On Bances's ideas concerning the theater, see his *Theatro de los theatros de los passados siglos.* Pról., ed. y notas de Duncan W. Moir (London, 1970). Also of great interest is Juan Manuel Rozas's "La licitud del teatro y otras cuestiones literarias en Bances Candamo, escritor límite," *Segismundo,* 1 (1965), pp. 247–73.

28. Quoted in A. A. Parker, *The Allegorical,* p. 21.

29. *Ibid.,* p. 23.

30. Ramón Esquer Torres, "Las prohibiciones de comedias y autos sacramentales en el siglo XVIII. Clima que rodeó a la Real Orden de 1765," *Segismundo,* 1 (1965), pp. 187–226. For a general study on the controversies of the theater, see Emilio Cotarelo y Mori, *Bibliografía de las controversias sobre la licitud del teatro en España* (Madrid, 1904), and also Edward M. Wilson, "Nuevos documentos sobre las controversias teatrales: 1650–1681," in *Actas del Segundo Congreso Internacional de Hispanistas,* ed. J. Sánchez Romeralo and N. Poloussen (Nijmegen, 1967), pp. 155–70.

# Selected Bibliography

### PRIMARY SOURCES

BUCK, VERA HELEN, ed. *Four Autos Sacramentales of 1590.* Iowa City: University of Iowa Studies, 1937.

CALDERÓN DE LA BARCA, PEDRO. *Obras Completas. Tomo III, Autos sacramentales.* Ed. A. Valbuena Prat. 2nd ed. Madrid: Aguilar, 1967.

GONZÁLEZ OLLÉ, FERNANDO, ed. "La *Farsa del Santísimo Sacramento,* anónima, y su significación en el desarrollo del auto sacramental," *Revista de Literatura,* 35 (1969), 127–65. Text of the play, pp. 142–62.

KEMP, ALICE BOWDOIN, ed. *Three Autos Sacramentales of 1590.* Toronto: 1936.

LÓPEZ DE YANGUAS, FERNÁN. *Obras dramáticas.* Ed. de F. González Ollé. Madrid: Espasa-Calpe, 1967.

SÁNCHEZ DE BADAJOZ, DIEGO. *Recopilación en metro (Sevilla, 1554).* Trabajos de seminario bajo la dirección de Frida Weber de Kurlat. Buenos Aires: Universidad de Buenos Aires, 1968.

TYRE, CARL ALLEN, ed. *Religious Plays of 1590.* Iowa City: University of Iowa Studies, 1938.

VALDIVIELSO, JOSÉ DE. *Teatro Completo.* Ed. de Ricardo Arias and Robert V. Piluso. 2 vols. Madrid: Isla, 1975–77.

VEGA CARPIO, LOPE FÉLIX DE. *Obras. VI Autos y coloqios.* I. Ed. y est. preliminar de M. Menéndez Palayo. Madrid: Atlas, 1963.

### SECONDARY SOURCES

AICARDO, J. M. "Autos anteriores a Lope de Vega," *Razón y Fe,* 5 (1903), 312–26; 6 (1903), 20–33; 201–14; 446–58; 7 (1903), 163–76. The author studies some important aspects of the *Códice de autos viejos.*

AUERBACH, ERICH. "Figura." In *Scenes from the Drama of European Literature.* New York: Meridian Books, 1959, pp. 9–76. Excellent study for the understanding of prefiguration and biblical allegory. Rpt: Gloucester, Mass., 1973.

BATAILLON, MARCEL. "Essai d'explication de l'Auto Sacramental," *Bulletin Hispanique,* 42 (1940), 193–212. Spanish translation

167

in his *Varia lección de clásicos españoles*. Madrid: Gredos, 1964, pp. 188–91. Probing essay which gave direction to many studies that followed.

CILVETI, ANGEL L. *El demonio en el teatro de Calderón*. Valencia: Albatros, 1977. This work studies the Devil and his multiple manifestations as an essential element in Calderón's *autos*.

DIETZ, DONALD THADDEUS. *The "Auto Sacramental" and the Parable in Spanish Golden Age Literature*. Chapel Hill, N.C.: Department of Romance Languages, 1973. Comprehensive study of the many *autos* dealing with the parables of the New Testament, written by several authors of different periods. Very useful for its comparative method.

FLECNIAKOSKA, JEAN-LOUIS. *La formation de l' "auto" religieux en Espagne avant Calderón (1550–1635)*. Montpellier: Paul Déhan, 1961. A complete reference work on the *autos*, their important themes, and the allegorical technique. Good bibliography included.

————. "Les conflicts tragiques dans l'auto religieux précaldéronien." In *Le théatre tragique*. Ed. J. Jacquot. Paris: Editions du Centre National de la Recherche Scientifique, 1962, pp. 107–17. An excellent study of the elements which contribute to dramatic situations in the *autos*.

FLETCHER, ANGUS. *Allegory. The Theory of a Symbolic Mode*. Ithaca, N.Y.: Cornell University Press, 1964. A good introduction to allegory with a substantial bibliography.

FOTHERGILL-PAYNE, LOUISE. *La alegoría en los autos y farsas anteriores a Calderón*. London: Támesis, 1977. A comprehensive study of allegorical technique and motifs before Calderón.

FRUTOS CORTÉS, EUGENIO. *La filosofía de Calderón en sus autos sacramentales*. Zaragoza: C.S.I.C., 1952. A basic study on the philosophical tenets in Calderón's *autos*.

GEWECKE, F. *Thematische Untersuchungen zu dem vor Calderonischen Auto Sacramental*. Geneva: Droz, 1974. This work is very helpful in the study of the themes in the *autos* before Calderón.

HANSON, R. P. C. *Allegory and Event. A Study of the Sources and Significance of Origen's Interpretation of Scripture*. Richmond, Va.: John Knox Press, 1959. One of the best studies on Origen's allegorical method of interpreting the Bible.

HARDISON, JR. O.B. *Christian Rite and Christian Drama in the Middle Ages*. Baltimore: Johns Hopkins Press, 1969. A basic work on the importance of the liturgy in early European theater.

LÁZARO CARRETER, FERNANDO, ed. *Teatro medieval.* 2nd ed. Madrid: Castalia, 1965. An excellent introduction to medieval Spanish theater.

PARKER, A. A. *The Allegorical Drama of Calderón.* Oxford: The Dolphin Book Co., 1943. The best introduction to the *autos* of Calderón, with an excellent analysis of three of them: *The Great Theater of the World, Belshazzar's Banquet,* and *Life Is a Dream.*

RUIZ LAGOS, MANUEL. "Una técnica dramática de Calderón: la pintura y el centro escénico," *Segismundo,* 2 (1966), 91–104. The author studies Calderón's use of paintings and stage decorations as an important part of the total spectacle.

SAGE, JACK. "Calderón y la música teatral," *Bulletin Hispanique,* 58 (1956), 275–300. This study examines the essential role of music in the plays of Calderón.

SANZOLES, FRAY MODESTO DE. "La alegoría como constante estilística de Lope de Vega en los autos sacramentales," *Revista de Literatura,* 16 (1959), 90–133. Lope's achievements and failures in the use of allegory are presented.

STERN, CHARLOTTE. "The Early Spanish Drama. From Medieval Ritual to Renaissance Art," *Renaissance Drama,* 6 (1973), 177–201. A good study on the need to consider the play as part of a larger spectacle. It is very relevant to the understanding of the *auto.*

VAGAGGINI, CYPRIAN, O.S.B. *Theological Dimensions of the Liturgy. A General Treatise on the Theology of the Liturgy.* Collegeville, Minn.: The Liturgical Press, 1976. The best treatise on the theological content of the liturgy and on the central role of the Eucharist in it.

VALBUENA PRAT, ANGEL. "Los autos sacramentales de Calderón (clasificación y análisis)," *Revue Hispanique,* 61 (1924), 1–302. One of the first and most serious attempts at classification of Calderón's *autos.*

VERY, FRANCIS GEORGE. *The Spanish Corpus Christi Procession: A Literary and Folkloric Study.* Valencia: Tipografía Moderna, 1962. Rich in information from many different sources.

WARDROPPER, BRUCE W. *Introducción al teatro religioso del siglo de oro.* Evolución del auto sacramental antes de Calderón. 2nd ed. Salamanca: Anaya, 1967. A good introduction to the study of the *auto,* with excellent insights into the aesthetics of the genre.

Staging of the Autos

LATORRE Y BADILLO, M. "Representación de los Autos Sacramentales en el período de su mayor florecimiento (1620 a 1681)," *Revista de Archivos, Bibliotecas y Museos,* 25 (1911), 189–211; 342–67; 26 (1912), 72–89; 236–62. The articles include many relevant documents of the period.

PÉREZ PASTOR, CRISTÓBAL. *Nuevos datos acerca del histrionismo español en los siglos XVI y XVII.* la serie. Madrid: Revista Española de Madrid, 1901. 2a. serie. Burdeos: Feret, 1914. This work contains many important data on the *autos.*

SHERGOLD, N. D. *A History of the Spanish Stage From Medieval Times Until the End of the Seventeenth Century.* Oxford: The Clarendon Press, 1967. The best work on the Spanish stage, with an excellent exposition of the role of the *autos* in it.

SHOEMAKER, W. H. *The Multiple Stage in Spain During the 15th and 16th Centuries.* Princeton: Princeton University Press, 1935. A good study, still very useful.

SHERGOLD, N. D. and J. E. VAREY. *Los autos sacramentales en Madrid en la época de Calderón, 1637–1681. Estudios y documentos.* Madrid: EDHIGAR, 1961. An important work on the staging of Calderón's *autos,* together with relevant documents.

————. "Autos sacramentales en Madrid hasta 1636." *Estudios Escénicos,* 4 (1959), 51–98.

Anthologies

ARIAS, RICARDO, ed. *Autos sacramentales.* 2 vols. México: Porrúa, 1977–78. The first volume includes works before Calderón. The second, only *autos* by Calderón.

GONZÁLEZ PEDROSO, EDUARDO, ed. *Autos sacramentales desde su origen hasta fines del siglo XVII.* Madrid: Atlas, 1952. Biblioteca de Autores Españoles, vol. 58. Originally published in 1865, this collection is still useful.

GONZÁLEZ RUIZ, NICOLÁS, ed. *Piezas maestras del teatro teológico español. I. Autos sacramentales.* Madrid: Editorial Católica, 1947. A useful anthology, but the texts are not too reliable.

ONRUBIA DE MENDOZA, JOSÉ, ed. *Trece autos sacramentales.* Barcelona: Bruguera, 1970.

SANVISENS, ALEJANDRO, ed. *Autos sacramentales eucarísticos*. Barcelona: Cervantes, 1952.

Autos in English Translation

BARNES, RICHARD G. *Three Spanish Sacramental Plays*. San Francisco: Chandler, 1969. They are Calderón's *Belshazzar's Feast*, Valdivielso's *The Bandit Queen*, and Lope's *For Our Sake*.
CALDERÓN DE LA BARCA, P. *The Sorceries of Sin*. Trans. Denis F. MacCarthy. London: Longman, 1861.
————. *Mysteries of Corpus Christi*. Trans. Denis F. MacCarthy. Dublin: James Duffy, 1867. They are *The Divine Philothea*, *Belshazzar's Feast*, and *The Poison and the Antidote*.
————. *The Great Theater of the World: From the Spanish of Calderón*. Trans. Richard C. Trench. London: J. W. Parker, 1856.

# Index